More Rebel Than Zen

Finding Motivation in Midlife

Adam Senex

The Sky Is Not the Limit….The Mind Is.

" In a world in which most of us are preoccupied with externals –
accumulating more stuff and building fake personas to fit every
situation. I consider my task with my books to be as a messenger,
someone that gives myself and others a gentle poke and to suggest
that maybe there are other ways to think about things and more
questions that need to be discovered and asked. Leading to yet
more questions.

My task is to create an interesting, healing and pleasurable art out
of self-examination and ultimately self-realization. This awareness
made available to people who, like me, are finding themselves
caught in the rigors and realizations involved in the process of
growing up as mature adults in the second part of life, having
assumed it would all get easier and that we were the finished
article. Having no guide and holding ourselves and significant
others to blame for being conned into believing we are fully matured
but in no way prepared for what lies before us in the second part of
life. Or for that matter what goes on behind our backs. If I can only
manage to persuade one other person to look at what may really be
going on in the world and inside of our hearts and minds, then I will
have done tremendously well."

Adam Senex

Contents

Getting Better

We often hear or read about tales of life changing retreats and defining moments when others have achieved the state of enlightenment. Rarely is a book written without the author claiming to have risen to another level. A level above normal consciousness. Becoming enlightened has been added to many others goals lists. The goal of ordinary people where it was once considered the domain of gurus and monks isolated on a mountain top in a far off and mysterious land. Where does that leave the rest of us that need to live in the real world where genuine sanctuaries are few and far between and the turbulent world now stalks us until we sleep and is waiting to leech onto us once more at first light? Whether we choose to accept it or not we are mind controlled throughout our real world existence.

Ironically there are many cases of even the most revered Buddhist monks attempting to deliver enlightenment to us in the real world only to fall victim to the very demons they seek to free us from. All too human failings. One dying from aids contracted by having sex with his followers and continuing to do so after having contracted the disease believing he was immune to the real world, with no thought for his partners. Another famously dying an alcoholic.

If these fates and countless others await even the best intentioned of us, then what is our purpose in this land of plenty? We are surrounded by shadow at every turn. Under such circumstances even the busiest of communities can feel like the loneliest mountain retreat. We are all ultimately alone.

My solution with the getting better series of books is more a strategy for getting better and staying motivated within the lives that we live moment to moment. One step at a time. Where might that lead us? Who knows but I do know that we have much potential that is vastly untapped and that is our inner space. Billions is spent on exploring outer space. I am suggesting that we explore inner space. A project that we can take on at whatever starting point and make progress. We are capable of changing the world simply by changing ourselves by overcoming fear and seeing through the lies that we are soaking up through the media on a day to day basis.

Stay strong, because things will get better. It might be stormy now, but it can't rain forever.
WWW.LIVELIFEHAPPY.COM

Learning by our mistakes and the mistakes of others, such as the well intentioned Buddhist gentlemen above, even myself and any person that you encounter on your journey. Any person within a similar process of attempting to give meaning to life assists us on our progress road. We are all searching for meaning and the truth about what goes on in life as yet mysteries undiscovered and also behind our backs knowingly by powers that seek to subtly dominate and control the human race. In this case what we don't know most definitely will hurt us. And is limiting us via mind control as I write.

Getting better across the whole of life is a noble life purpose and the perfect way to fill the days of our lives. A life purpose of transcending what comes before us. Relationships, health and fitness, success, motivation, love and getting to know ourselves better are all exciting ways to get better and there are more, many more. I hope that this book challenges your thought process and changes your life for the better. But above all I hope you now realise that you are not alone on your mission, although your mission is unique, knowing others share your journey helps making achieving goals that much easier.

So there we have it. Our goal is to get better in every way we can moment to moment and day to day. By getting better we will change the world, our world, this beautiful planet will be saved for generations to come. Look no further for your life purpose, getting better and transcending what it means to be human is all the life purpose we will ever need. Why not start now?

Introduction - More Rebel Than Zen

I was on my mission to become enlightened when I first began to write professionally. If being totally honest I thought, I was doing pretty well and I would be one with the universe quite soon.

Others would ask "what do you write about?" I always seemed to struggle with a short answer and never felt that I could do justice to what I felt about my writing in a limited time frame. They wanted a summing up, a category that was contained in their head into which I would neatly fit. I would resist being pigeon holed and just ended up seeming as though I didn't know what I was writing about. And that is closer to the truth most of the time than any genre pigeon hole. Even my *Great Body Bible by The Fitness Wizards* did not really fit particularly neatly into any category although it can be found in the health and fitness or bodybuilding genres. There is much contained within its pages that transcends the genre.

I next began to answer that I was a spiritual writer but that did not fit at all. I even wondered if I should change to fit a particular genre but I didn't wonder for long. I was not fitting in just so I could be pigeon holed. As usual throughout my life I did not fit, there was no category or label for me to get comfortable with.

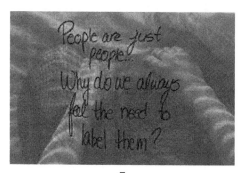

After much thought about this often asked question – that came after what do you do? I began using a more considered answer -

> **"I write about awareness, progress, getting better and how that might work for us all in the real world. My writing by necessity is probably more rebel than Zen** *due to the numerous discoveries by other authors of what might be happening behind our backs. I attempt to map personal progress despite all of our obstacles. I write to motivate, inspire and teach optimism in a very difficult world. I cover all aspects of life from health and fitness, work, relationships and everything in between. Getting better in the real world – whatever that might be!"*

The bold type is the abbreviated version for a conversation in passing.

This answer, arrived at after much deliberation and soul searching summed up both my life purpose personally and the purpose of my writing and communications with others which includes my own reading. The more rebel than Zen comment was one of those that was instantly catchy and has found its way to the title of this book. We would all like to be perfectly Zen a calm amongst the turbulent world and that was my initial intention with my writing. 100% constructive, positive and optimistic throughout it all but it soon became blatantly clear that there is much going on behind our backs and that approach would be unrealistic and quite frankly unworkable in a world that has many demons and not enough heroes and angels. If we wish to get better, it can't begin with ignoring anything that may make us uncomfortable. There is much in human society that will make us very uncomfortable indeed. I will signpost books to read for you to understand more fully to what I may be referring. And I have a website that lists the top personal development books – www.adamsenex.com .But you will need a very open mind and to fully understand that much of what you think you know now is programming.

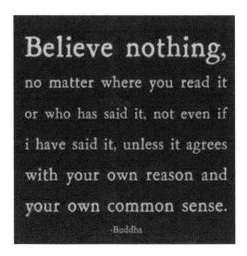

I am still optimistic and amazed at how limited our lives are before we choose to become more aware. Make no mistake it is a choice. Our world is an amazing place filled with both good and evil at every turn and it is the purpose of each and every human being to transcend what has come before. To discard the shackles that even now hold us into a limited existence. Each one of us is responsible for the evolution or destruction of the human race. Doing nothing is not an option.

My vote is for us to rise above the evil holding us down beginning with ourselves. All we have to do is change ourselves. Becoming aware is the start, progressing from wherever we are now is the next step. When we all do this it leads to the betterment of the entire human race as the higher resonance behaviours spread through the morphic field to influence others. We can change the world by simply changing what is normal behaviour and thought for human beings. Sadly, the same can be said for spreading evil and the race is on to choose one over the other and nurture the right choice, the only choice.

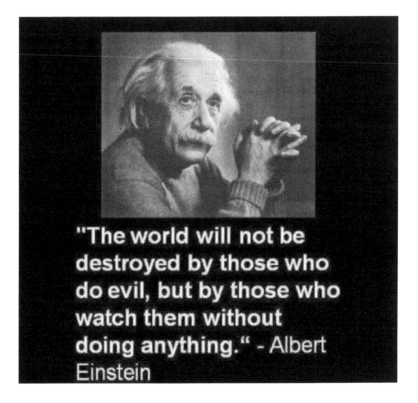

There is much love on this planet. The planet is also plagued with evil at every turn. Just watch the news but don't believe any of what is said. The truth will never be found on the television. Experts are wheeled out to bolster lies, science amongst the good it has accomplished has become a tool for manipulation. Science is a valuable tool used to spin whatever yarn our oppressors wish us to believe. Naivety combined with believing our programmed minds is our greatest obstacle. Maybe belittling so called conspiracy theories is their greatest weapon the same way as the scared school boy uses humour to make himself popular. Believing our rulers are benevolent is a mistake. Believing that conspiracy theories are lies and the news is truth is laughable but that is where we are at in our world. We are being hoodwinked and it is time to wake up and question the what, where, who, how and why we are being controlled. By becoming as much a rebel as we are Zen we can get better. In a society where the seven deadly sins have become the blue print for success we have our work cut out. I will grant you that the truth does take some change in beliefs from what we are programmed to accept as the truth of our existence and that is the beauty of the crime against us. We are programmed to want them to act for us and believe that they have our best interests at heart. They do not.

All I can say to that is to start and read as much as you can and sit through it no matter that your chatter box is telling you that it is pure fantasy it will get easier and then you can decide for yourself what might be real. The more you read the more things start piecing together in your mind and the realities of your world will change forever. However, the solution does not, it still begins and ends with you and your mind. A mind that you are setting free from its programming into a world that will shock and amaze you to the point of disbelief and gradually a shift in your world view will happen. A shift towards a truth that you have built for yourself despite the mind control bombardment from the malevolent forces within society.

We must feed our good wolf and be aware of our bad wolf and even have some fun knowing that we contain everything inside for both good and evil. It is our choices that ultimately decide our fate and will decide the fate of this beautiful planet. Aligning our wolves is a good place to begin. Letting them coexist rather than trying to be all good is the solution.

An old Cherokee told his grandson, "My son, there is a battle between two wolves inside us all.

One is Evil. It is Anger, Jealousy, Greed, Resentment, Inferiority, Lies, & Ego. The other is Good. It is Joy, Peace, Love, Hope, Humility, Kindness, Empathy, & Truth."

The boy thought about it, and asked, "Grandfather, which wolf wins?"

The old man quietly replied, "The one you feed."

Your world view will become exactly that YOUR world view and will be ever changing as your read and experience your life. This is a fluid process, a process of discovery and then rediscovery. You will need a mind wide open mind and the ability to quite happily contradict yourself when new insights arise for you. You will develop a hunger for discovery and a curious questioning mind that will constantly look for findings that sit well with you and your developing and ever changing world view.

I suppose the question is can our collective good wolf save the human race and this planet? We can do our best.

Let's get started....

Read – Read – Read

I have put reading first because as far as I am concerned if I had not rediscovered reading I would still be suffering in my automated ignorance and have no real aim in my life. You can read about my change of life attitude in my book -Dazed & Confused.

Now I am still ignorant but I have found the perfect balance for my ignorance in an opposite, knowledge. I will not say wisdom because that depends on what one does with the knowledge gained and the jury is still out on that one. Yet another example of a progressive move towards wholeness by uniting opposites in a way that feels just right. My new saying is "It's always both" – the answer is always both.

Of all of the possible paths of progression that I will mention and those that I will miss including, reading rates highly because of a book's infinite ability to change who we are as readers. Ignorance is suffering and whilst we will never cease to learn and always be ignorant reading goes a long way to balancing ignorance. And reading a wide range of books also keeps our minds wide open to new and ever more mind boggling ideas that eventually become the facts. Albeit such facts have a relatively short reign as facts. Nevertheless, the process continues. Fact is revealed and eventually superseded by new fact and so on.

Reading can become a search for buried treasure that almost always produces a treasure of some sort. The more skilled we become at aligning our book choices in our search for knowledge, meaning and ultimately wisdom with where we are at that unique moment in time, the more productive our search becomes. However, there are those amazing moments when a book we have attempted to tackle but failed in the challenge, maybe not understanding and managing even a chapter, when picked up again sometime in the future becomes an experience of clarity and understanding. Why? Because we have changed due to our reading between the two attempts. What a fantastic feeling and evidence of the benefit of reading and progress. It is a wonderful example of the idea that when the student is ready the teacher will appear. The teacher is always present inside our books.

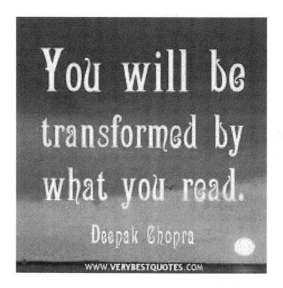

It is also clear from the historical incidents of tyrants and institutions destroying and burning books when wishing to gain control and produce docile subjects, that books have the power to encourage original thinking, allowing us the freedom to choose the thoughts we like (opinions). It is so much easier to control the docile to think and act "normally" by conditioning them with the thoughts and ideas considered best for them and as such normal at the same time denying access to the knowledge that can free minds. Books are that powerful. I think the internet has a role to play for our rulers in turning people away from books for greater control on the web.

Remember this quote from my first book in this series Dazed & Confused -

> *It is only by enlightened people that this book can be read; the ordinary man is not made for such knowledge; philosophy will never be his lot. Those who say that there are truths which must be hidden from the people need not be alarmed; the people do not read; they work six days of the week, and on the seventh go to the inn. In a word, philosophical works are made only for philosophers, and every honest man must try to be a philosopher, without pluming himself on being one.*

—Voltaire

Have things changed since Voltaire's time. I doubt it. The information fed to the masses (us) is now more automated than ever and the behaviour more robotic. The way to freedom is through books. But they may as well be hidden for they do not get read to any extent. The ruling classes are not even bothered about censoring as they are confident in the masses laziness and indifference to reading.

In our current climate the ruling classes don't have to be so concerned as people are either too distracted by television, phone and a million others gadgets to read at all or read hedonistic fairy tales and celebrity biographies or out of context quotes from the web. The real treasure is hidden beneath so much meaningless crap that very few truth seekers are up to the task of breaking from the norms and allowing the reading of quality books to join the dots and add some depth and meaning to life. Good books provide an endless search for answers and more questions, a good author will always leave a paper trail via references and bibliographies that will advance your progress. The ideal situation is to have so many books on your mental list and waiting to be read on your shelves or chosen e-reader that you feel you will not live long enough to gain the progress they will undoubtedly create inside of you by expanding and opening your mind in awe and wonder.

I have a kindle reader and I also buy physical books. The reader is fantastic and fast and convenient. I can have a new book in seconds. However, for me the feel of a good book cannot be replaced, with my e-reader I view all I need one page at a time. But with the live book I get the feel of the blood, sweat and tears of the author and I hold that entire experience in my hand. It is difficult to explain but my relationship and connection to the actual physical book is a much richer experience for me. Maybe it is also a resistance to technology as always being considered progress when I believe there are many instances when technology actually regresses the human organism. Technology disconnects us from being physically bound to each other and all that there is. It is impersonal. As always the answer may be in the acceptance of both in our lives. A more discerning choice of when to accept new technology and how to use it to enhance our lives. Currently, technology is taking over lives. The responsibility is ours to be strong enough not to get dragged along by the current of all that is new is better. Moderation has always been a good path to follow. I will always use book and e-reader. For me, a new or used book arriving with the mail is a moment of excitement and anticipation to rival any other. This is from a man that had not read a serious book from cover to cover until my mid-forties. I now read at least 1 or 2 books each week and cannot imagine not reading or how I managed to live previously never having read a book. I was that docile citizen, ingesting only what was fed to me through my culture and the media. A prisoner of society. My progress in the last ten years has been astronomical. Whilst not regretting the first half of my life, I feel I have only begun to choose the life that I wish to lead for the last decade. Books have opened my eyes to life and helped to explain my former life in wonderful ways. Books bring laughter and tears. Books provide optimism and motivation for any future, as knowing is what we all desire. With books we can all progress, expand and grow continuously without being informed what to think and subtly led to our opinions, which are not really ours at all. Reading keeps minds wide open and helps us to come to terms with the paradox of life once narrow mindedness becomes a thing of the past.

I always knew deep inside that I should read but considered magazines and newspapers to be sufficient. When I decided I wanted to or needed to read seriously, my life was in a state and I needed something, anything to give me the passion to live life. My passion for life had left me and I was helplessly surviving from turbulent day to turbulent day. I was seriously considering whether it was all really worth it. However, out of the blue came a book, a self-help book that whilst serious readers would feel was commercial trash, it served to turn my life around with its extremely over the top positive message. As a starting point this book was perfect for my state of mind at that time in my life. I changed my whole life on the strength of this book and have never looked back. The change made was not external although my external world changed. My world changed because I began to change myself, to progress every day where possible and my inner changes shaped my choices and decisions that affected my material world.

When I decided or was led to wanting or needing to read I remember not being able to focus very well and counting pages to see how far until I could stop at a completed chapter or how far I had read. I was unable to be mindful for very long, restless and clock watching. This was an extreme challenge and one that I see in many others today, an inability to focus. I feel this is bought on by our fast paced world setting a tempo inside of us that is unable to slow down without addictive distractions such as television, food, the internet, not to mention drugs and alcohol. The ability to read in a slow and relaxed state is paramount to remaining human through the assault to our senses from the 21st century. If we want to become more mindful, which is the fad of the moment, then learning to sit quietly and read books with no rush is the ideal place to begin. I know of people that go to workshops and retreats often but cannot read a book. Just sit in the silence and read a book. Initially our egos, feeling threatened will try everything to stop us but eventually we win through and the ego sees the benefit of reading to the organism and inner harmony is restored. Silence is a vital ingredient and once we learn to read with pleasure and our sense of time disappears as with any pastime that we engage in fully, It becomes timeless.

In the early days I don't think I really read much of the book I had in my hands. I had to learn to focus, concentrate and engage rather than just scan the pages aimlessly. Nowadays I am much more aware (mindful) of whether I am actually reading or not and I invariably talk over what I read with Julie or myself to reinforce the new ideas and thoughts created by the words.

I believe any of us living in these high tech, fast paced times can be A.D.H.D. to a certain degree, living lives bombarded with information, flicking our attention from fidgety task to fidgety task and never really focusing our attention on one task very well. A premium has been placed on the myth of multi-tasking to the detriment of doing any tasks well. The fact is we all have a similar amount of information processing space and we are limited by our 5 – 9 bits or chunks of capacity for conscious short term attention. This information is fragile and is lost with distraction or the passing of time unless repeated and reinforced. Multi-tasking is dividing that focused attention capacity and will affect how well each task is performed until the tasks become subconscious behaviours.

Reading is best undertaken in comfort and silence. If music is playing you will be either listening or reading, each will be in competition with the other. I do play music at times but I am aware that when I read the music is ignored. So why bother and risk losing focus on good music or a good book.

A good book is mindfulness meditation and as such the effort to maintain focus changes your brain, helping to offset some of the turbulent distractions of normal life. Simplifying the word mindfulness is "to concentrate well on one thing at a time". Another good phrase is "attend and stay". Reading fits the bill. I joke with the some of the young men that I mentor that I will be teaching them to read. They look at me with horror and offended until they realise they can't focus for more than a few minutes and after blaming the book and everything else external to them they come to accept the fact that they have never focused on a complete page, let alone a complete book. Knowing that just as I discovered in myself they read magazines, web sites, quotes and watch video and television clips. Once they realise they begin the extremely difficult process of overcoming that prevalent conditioned behaviour by learning to be present in the moment to read, think and progress as individuals. This is a massive challenge with temptation everywhere. I have watched many fail and just give up, never to know the undervalued joy of reading and progressing our minds. However, I am confident that once the seed is planted that as we mature we come to terms more with these challenges and progress accordingly.

I had a discussion with Julie, my wife recently about how long the ideal book should be. One of my books was over 750 pages "The Great Body Bible" by The Fitness Wizards (Julie and I). This book is huge and would not be an easy read on a lap. The result of our discussion was that we thought books should be shorter (-200 pages) to accommodate those just taking up the challenge. I have memories of preferring short books as ones I could complete. Completing a book is satisfying, as with any short term goal success. Julie thought that books should be short, interesting and motivate the reader in their search for knowledge, meaning and progress. I now search for longer books if I have a choice but as Julie pointed out I am not a 'normal' reader. The length of the book you hold in your hands will give you an idea as to the conclusion we arrived at.

Reading induces tears of joy and tears of sadness. Through Bibliotherapy reading fills in the gaps in the meaning in our lives, gaps we didn't even realise were there until they are filled by the wisdom of another. Reading introduces the richness of language and words, making words barely comprehensible previously become clear and enlightening in the time to come as a new you emerges from your contact with the pages. It can be a difficult journey, a journey worthy of a hero. Your own personal hero's journey, every bit as exciting as those you will read about and to know and relate to intimately. We are all embroiled in a hero's journey called life, a journey toward wholeness. A journey with a full list of characters and adventures both inside of us and outside of us, if we can just step back and witness it.

To progress a personal philosophy for life is not possible without a unique reading journey being led by intuition and curiosity. Normally such a perceived philosophy is copied and taken from others without books. A readymade blueprint for living life handed to us and never really fitting the unique individuals we are or allowing for the fulfilment of the amazing potential we each possess.

A life view is a subtle raising of experience into personalised thoughts, memories and theories. Eventually following a period of incubation, they condense and form into a flexible life philosophy, one that is unique for each of us. Even in the unlikely event of two of us reading exactly the same books the life philosophies would still be unique as our perception and processing of the material will be unique. A philosophy is not an abstract collection of thoughts for their own sake such as those handed to individuals by institutions but it is rather the ripening of conversation, reading and experience into open minded thoughts. These thoughts become wedded to every day decisions and subject to ongoing personal analysis. Such ideas become part of our progressive identity and allow us confidence in work and life decisions. They are never final, they provide a new starting point for further wonder and exploration that reaches through science, religion and spiritual practice into the mysteries that saturate human experience. Insight will continue to come until some level of wisdom is achieved. Wisdom is arguably the achieved harmony of intellects longing for truth and the psyches acceptance of the nature of the human condition through soulful experience. Wisdom is the fusion of intellect with soul. Reading progresses this fusion towards wholeness.

Above all else reading teaches us to value our ignorance, to know the value of harmonising ignorance with knowledge (maybe wisdom) to rest in a place that is just right. The realisation that with all of the learning, expansion and progress we still know very little. This mixing of pride and humility will keep us grounded and in the perfect state of mind to learn and progress for as long as we are able.

No matter how busy you may think you are, you must find time ———— for ————

READING

———— or ————

surrender yourself to self-chosen ignorance.

-Confucius

Stop – Sense – Go

If you are a busy person this exercise will help you to balance your psyche (soul) whilst fitting your busy lifestyle. It would be better not to be so busy but there are times when we all take on too much when challenged by our culture to conform to standard expectations. This is how we begin to fight back, by seeking out small mindful moments.

Pick a sense, any sense. You may use any sense you favour or vary them across your day to suit the situation.

Touch, see, listen, taste or smell. Whichever you are using – ATTEND & STAY – for a precious moment.

I favour listening with eyes closed. An example from my life is to close my eyes and focus on my ticking clocks, total silence or birdsong, depending on where I am. I even meet a bird on my walks that mimics a fire engine siren. When I first moved into the area I went exploring amongst the labyrinth of houses and I got a little lost until I heard my fire engine siren mimicking friend and I found my way home.

With eyes closed I relax and listen and immediately feel the experience of being present throughout the whole of my body. I ATTEND & STAY just briefly. Another I have used in the past is when arriving at any destination in a car to turn everything off in one go and attend to the contrasting silence. It is a moment of absolute heaven before I move back into the flow of the turbulent life that western culture requires us to lead.

I experience the same with the initial taste of good food, particularly after fasting. The odour of coconut products and various shrubs and flowers, I can often be found with my head in an aromatic bush (ooer!). The sight of birds of prey in flight is trance inducing as are many other spontaneous moments throughout nature. I attend fully and stay for as long as I am able, mostly too long as it is difficult to escape once you are bewitched. I even close my eyes while stroking the dogs and if you have a very good friend, in my case Julie, one can touch and stroke the others face and both the toucher and touched enjoy the experience of the other being present in the same moment. The other will know if you are not present the experience will not be the same.

Someday everything will make perfect sense.

So, for now, laugh at the confusion, smile through the tears and keep reminding yourself that everything happens for a reason.

> Your five senses tells you
> the truth, your touch, your
> smell, your sight, your taste
> & your hearing...your sixth
> sense tells you the
> infinitive truth...gut
> feelings, never ignore!!
> – Morris Fox

We tend to abuse, neglect and overload our senses in the 21st century, these moments teach us a new appreciation of something we, as developing humans have come to take for granted in our desensitised states.

Rediscovering our senses and boosting our human experience throughout the day is a pleasure that you will not forget.

Just remember! Whatever the moment. ATTEND & STAY even for the briefest precious moment.

Peace to you all.

 Online Dictators

There seems to be a belief that discussions need to have a winner and a loser. Added to that seems to be the belief that within any topic that there is only one universal truth for everyone and people with opinions not matching the most aggressive participant's opinions must then be battered into submission. It is to all intents and purposes a meaningless and mindless power struggle in which often reasonably intelligent individuals abuse others. Bullying by any other name. On any given subject there are infinite subjective truths for individuals based on their ultimate uniqueness in this world. Differences of religion, culture, gender, geography, personal experience and the list goes on, ensuring that no two people will ever have the same truth on any topic. This is subjective truth - truth for the individual subject. There are no universal truths.

So where does this leave discussion forums for them to be an effective place for the acquisition of knowledge and ultimately personal progress and growth?

I will use a true story to illustrate this point. In the 1960's in France there were very serious student riots in which the whole country went on strike in support of the students. Prominent academics such as Jean Paul Sartre and Michel Foucault were heavily involved. To cut a long story short eventually President De Gaulle was seen as the victor and the riots were quelled. This is where the story gets interesting. Michel Foucault some years later when writing about his technologies of dominance and governmentality used the incident to show how the people can make a difference and exert their freedom. To many the students cause was lost, however within ten years all that they had asked for had become reality. How? The seeds of change had been planted and the new thoughts and ideologies had been incorporated within the psyche of the country. Given time to mature given time to develop without undue pressure after the initial unrest the thought processes spread to include people in high places and through time the very ideas that they had fought against had become their own. The seeds had been planted. The riots and unrest could be seen as the planting period and the eventual realisation of the ideals, the harvest.

The conclusion here is that in order to make a difference to any thought process one must first realise that we are constantly thinking until the day we die and our thought processes evolve accordingly. Attempting to batter others to seeing your point of view is futile at best. However, a well ordered and positive discussion with many viewpoints and opinions and an acceptance of others views, can and will result in a growth in the total intellect of that discussion. With this approach everyone wins. In summary an acceptance of each individual as an individual with a unique opinion and not a robot to be programmed with the same opinions as all other robots.

 Communicating

I vaguely remember from my time studying psychology that when humans communicate, only 7 per cent is via the words spoken. The rest is subtle body language, tone, and an almost-instinctual ability humans have for relating to one another. There is much more going on than the transfer of mere words. I have a feeling that humans are becoming less connected to nature, the planet, and each other, even though we are supposedly in the golden age of communication. How can we relate to other humans using the full human ability to communicate when we are doing it through technology, much of which just involves the exchange of words (only 7 per cent)? Is this just another wedge human beings are driving between themselves and their true nature? Are we evolving to become more machine than human? If the words become all there is to relating to others, will we open ourselves up to insincerity and lies? Will future generations lose the ability to really communicate? To have gut feelings? To intuitively know when something is not right, or vice versa?

This reminds me again of a slice of Buddhist wisdom that states that the most important time is now, and the most important person is the one you are with. Why? Because nothing else exists. The past is exactly that, and the future is an illusion until it becomes the now. There will be those who argue that technology is just the next stage in human communication evolution. I am not one of them. I believe humans should communicate unaided by technology; we may even find there is an evolutionary path to be found in that direction. Maybe we can enhance our natural abilities, or develop new abilities lying dormant in our human makeup.

I have had many spooky moments. We have all had those freaky moments when we knew the phone would ring or were thinking of someone and they appeared. At times we feel that we are causing things to happen. Coincidence? Maybe, but wouldn't it be nice to be patient and uncover our natural abilities before we lose all instinctive, intuitive abilities to our reliance on technology? We may be severing a vital connection to our human evolution that we can never rediscover. Do we control technology, or is it controlling us? I know what I think, but I am fighting back. It's not that I want to eradicate all technology but to realise there can be too much of a good thing. I would like to take more time to look at the future consequences of technology before we get too excited and reliant on it. There are already too many humans whose perception is that they cannot live without technology or, even sadder, of course they could, but why should they? That means they are being controlled by technology and the producers of that technology. Maybe human beings are not destined to be the masters of the universe after all; that title will be awarded to their high-tech machine-behaviour dictators.

hear no evil, see no evil, speak no evil, post no evil

Creativity vs Money

In modern times it can be hard to comprehend where our sources of individual creativity are going to come from. We are in danger of categorising and labelling any talent and making it conform to a recognised-as-normal idea of the creative, in order that it can be sold for profit. No longer are we presented with something unique and different so we have to both strive to understand its uniqueness and be comfortable with anything different. Are we in danger of losing our individual creative talent to either the lure of money or to the approval of society? This can be seen in the arts, sports and, I am guessing, in most areas, as a general sign of the dampening of creativity to fit the market and to earn profit. When one asks creative people to play by the rules, to follow a blueprint, or to follow a game plan, more often than not they begin to lose their driving passion. But the reality is that they have to pay the bills, unless they can get an extremely patient sponsor or a sponsor who doesn't want an immediate return or any return at all – a sponsor with an unconditional belief in the talent or ideas of the artist. This would indeed be very rare in these days of "What's in it for me?"

Creativity vs. Innovation

Creativity is the process of developing new or interesting ideas.

Innovation is the process of transforming creative ideas into valuable or profitable solutions.

Do such people (sponsors) exist? For most of us, the answer is probably not, other than maybe spouses or family members with faith in their loved one's ability. How many readers would compromise their creative talent for a big payday? In sports, maybe thirty or forty years ago, youngsters played their sport because they loved it and wanted to emulate their heroes at their chosen sport. These days, youngsters are more likely to have a rich celebrity sports person as a role model, as much because of their celebrity lifestyle as any sporting reasons. This has been proven not to increase motivation extrinsically (for the riches) but rather to stifle and distract from any intrinsic motivation (passion). Authors in the book charts I noticed at Christmas time are mostly celebrities aiming to milk every single avenue of their celebrity status for as much profit as they can. There's probably not a classic to be found amongst the cookery, fitness, and autobiographical books. Why does anyone subscribe to the cheap trash on sale? Because it is cheap and has a celebrity on the cover?

My final question has to be this one: Are we willing to settle for mediocrity in order that somebody can profit? It could be argued that it is the state of play currently. Even more of a worry would be that we are getting what we want but have faded so far culturally that we feel what is on offer constitutes art for us now. I say we and us, but I personally have no doubt that what is on offer for the general public generally in no way constitutes art as I recognise it. I find myself having to search harder and harder for a decent book, a challenging read. I want something that stimulates the grey matter long after I have read the book for the first time and leaves me knowing that I will read that book again, it being impossible to take in every little nuance contained within in just one read. These books are always from a different era. They are priceless snippets of another's mind. Where is the intellectually challenging contemporary material?

It may sound as if I feel there is no room for the current material being sold. To the contrary, I know that if it is being sold then there must be a need created for it. My problem is that the market is narrowing so much that other, less commercially viable yet culturally relevant, material may be vanishing into the mists of time. Consumers in the twenty-first century are more often buying what they are told to buy, the same as others are buying. What takes the least effort to appreciate? There is too much choice but very little variety. Do all the bestselling books actually get read, or do people buy them as the trendy item to have an interest and never actually get round to reading them? I don't understand how everyone's literary tastes can suddenly be the same, unless there is a large element of having to have the same as other people included in the scheme of things. Maybe purchases are based on finding out what all the fuss is about, or being able to say they own that book, the same as others. Maybe it's a case of possession rather than appreciation.

Under the Surface

I have a very good friend who freely discusses his life with me, and I have his permission to talk anonymously about his relationship with his wife here in this book. His wife is of the same mind. She is perfectly happy that I relate their problems to my readers. They feel that their story may help others to persevere with relationships rather than go hunting for a perfection that we all know does not exist. Any other person observing my friend's life and relationship to his wife would think that they have the perfect marriage. I use the word perfect here even though we all know that perfection in human terms can never exist. However, to outward glances, they have a model relationship to be envied. I have witnessed first-hand complete strangers complimenting them on their perfect relationship. They are fit, reasonable looking, and the best of friends. They share the same interests and live what seems to be a perfectly complementary life with one another. They had their problems early in their relationship, as most people do when marriage is more the next stage in life rather than a real commitment. ("What's next? We get married now, like everyone else does." It's no surprise so many marriages fail.)

This couple have been together for over thirty years in total. What can be so wrong with this perfection? I love seeing them together; they seem so comfortable, so made for each other. He worships her and does so much for her. One would never think they had any secrets from one another. They talk so openly; maybe she is a little more reserved when it comes to expressing real feelings. They are in total agreement about everything. That includes the problem infecting their life, a problem that has bought them so much suffering.

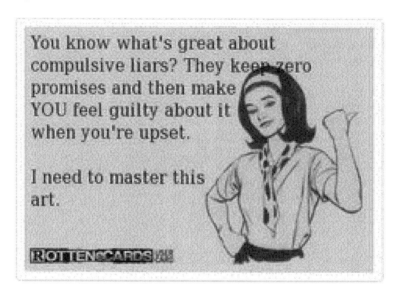

He can't trust her, no matter how hard he tries, because she is or was a compulsive liar. She has betrayed him so often and lied so much that he can no longer tell the truth from the lies. Each time she says that she will tell no more lies, another lie is about to surface. Most of the lies are of a sexual-betrayal nature, but there are all sorts of other needless lies scattered amongst the others. Once a sequence of lies begins, other lies are needed to make the earlier lies seem true. When I talk to them both, she can't explain why she lies, and she hates it that she does. She knows that she is hurting him every day. There is nothing she could tell him that he would not forgive, but this lying is like a torture, they both agree. The amazing thing is logically she can see the solution but there seems to be a part of her that acts independently, maybe her shadow side.

"You can always tell when he's lying – his lips move!"

Ironically, she is not a liar in other areas of her life; in work and professionally spheres he has noted she is the model of honesty and integrity. He sees their entire thirty years together as a past of lies, and he finds not having a real past very disturbing. He often blames himself as not creating the correct environment for truth. They have worked away from each other over the years, and he can't help but wonder what he doesn't know. He places such value on loyalty and feels he does not have a loyal wife; for him that is a substantial loss to his possible bond with her. Every day she goes to work and he knows he can't allow himself to trust her. Moreover, he never will. Does anyone ever really trust someone who has lied to them?

He says that he sees his life with her exactly as others see it, until he sits and analyses it carefully, and then he feels he is married to both an angel and the devil. Still, he feels that the positive side of the relationship and her endless (false) promises to change are more than enough for him to stay. "Better the devil you know", Hope springs eternal", and other such clichés spring to mind. A mixture of love and the hope of change is very powerful. It's amazing how one can suffer for the possibility of total perfection. They laugh, but I know that they both feel an element of truth in his words when he quotes those old faithful lines, "Count your blessings" and "For better or worse".

I have a newfound respect for their relationship, as perfection is easy to live with, but to attain what they have under the special circumstances is quite remarkable. He says that maybe they are paying for their relationship being so good at other times and in many other ways. This is the price, the dark shadow waiting to eclipse his light each time he allows himself to think rationally. I think that those balancing-the-books type of thoughts make it easier for him to deal with the horror of their situation.

Divorce courts are full of couples that run away at the first sign of having to work at a relationship. They hope, and often genuinely believe, that perfection awaits them elsewhere. In reality, it doesn't exist. They are searching for a fairy-tale romance, for a relationship as told by the movies and all those commercial enterprises that stand to gain from selling one side of the love phenomena. My friends are in it for the long haul, they are full of hope and optimism. I hope they conquer their demons. To lose a loved one's trust is indeed a tragic loss. Often it's a loss suffered without thinking of the consequences (that word again). Do not too easily lose the trust of anyone; it is more valuable than you realise.

Many couples work for years developing and earning each other's trust just to lose that same trust in the most trivial way, with some unimportant nonsense. That same nonsense can spell the end of the relationship, because with one lie the whole affair changes; at that moment one is changing the course of the past, present, and future. Imagine all that one has said in the past has been believed, but now that belief is cast under a shadow of doubt. One's whole life then becomes filled with doubt about what is true and what is false. It's a horrible way to live. The relationship will never be the same again. Maybe the golden rule applied here would make good sense. Treat others as you yourself would expect to be treated. It's not as easy as it sounds, but it's worth considering if you are involved in any kind of deceit and are seeking some peace of mind.

 ## Social Retards and Android Invasion

Many of you are very aware of my passionate feelings about the way our society is heading and my fear that future generations are becoming more machine than human or, at the least, hopelessly dependent on machines and technology to live their lives. We are at that point now. It touches lives either a little or a lot and will take over human existence unless there is an awakening within individuals or the whole human collective, meaning the entire herd changes direction.

The Death of Conversation

I have had many strange experiences, including mothers pulling prams up high curbs, baby dangerously threatened with the very real threat of being tipped into traffic but refusing to let go of the phone that they are talking on constantly, even in potentially dangerous situations. How can any conversation be that damned important? Many babies in pushchairs will have the lasting memory of a blank face staring at a phone, texting, as they look for facial features and communicate thus from their view out onto the world. Human beings' first important moments will be full of Mum and Dad being absorbed in their technology and ignoring them.

The art of conversation is dying!! All anybody does is text. I love talking to someone face to face!!

whisper

But let me tell you about my strangest experience yet. It was a beautiful sunny day, and the birds were singing. It felt good to be alive. I was walking through a park close to the town centre, on the path that runs straight as an arrow down one side. In the distance, I could hear and see a fast moving "thing" coming in my direction. It was stepping fast, both hands connected in front by way of a piece of technology, head down, designer clothing from head to toe, and emitting clicking noises from what must be the control panel for this particular android. It kept coming. I did not move to the side, by way of an experiment. I am 6′ 4″ and about 18 stone (120 kg). I could have been seen from the moon. I wanted to see how conscious the android was of what was happening in the world around it. The android kept on coming. At the last minute, I shouted, "Look out!" The android started, swerved, uttered the word sorry, and kept on going on a new path. I shook my head. This was the closest thing I have encountered yet to something much less than human. This is not okay. It is funny, but this person was not in the slightest connected to humanity or the world around him.

It would be too easy to dismiss this as an isolated incident. On the same day, a friend of mine travelled with work colleagues, in a large, comfortable automobile, to a destination about two hours away. I would have thought it was normal for them to chat and socialise with each other. My friend is also a neo Luddite and as such has no yearning for gadgets to replace humans at times like these. She would like nothing better than to see public use of mobile phones banned except in emergencies. She was horrified to report that for two hours solid, every person on board had his or her gadgets in hand and did not utter a word to each other. She thought the return journey might offer more in the way of social interaction. Nothing for another two hours – and this is the golden age of communication? Crisis? What crisis? My friend thought it a very rude way to behave, but she did say that it is normal behaviour these days for many people to ignore any person they are with who is not a close friend or family member and connect instead with their technology. Charming, and just a little bit worrying.

 Yesterday

I have to tell you about something that happened yesterday. My day started with Julie dropping me off at the break of day beside the woods, while she went off to Nottingham to work. I spent an hour in the woods and then walked the two miles back home for breakfast and to feed the birds. I had oatmeal, and Jake and Smudge had their usual morning treat of rice pudding. I settled down to work, and the dogs curled up on the sofa for a nap; so far, so good. My mum sent her usual text. Put the kettle on, she told me, as she was on her way to visit.

As we had just sat down to drink our tea and chat about what had happened in our lives since we last met, I heard a knock at the door. It was a lady whom I will call Betty. Betty has lived in the same house for what seems like the whole of my life. Betty is a friend in her early eighties; she lives alone and has never really got over the breakup of her marriage to Bill which happened many years ago.

Bill still owns the house she lives in and visits every day, doing all he can to help. Whether that is conscience or his never really letting go totally, I don't know. I am not a relationship expert, but I have witnessed many times couples splitting up and the one that has left not being able to give up totally the original partner. I have always thought this is unfair; they are having their cake and eating it, as the saying goes. By being so close, they are preventing the other ever getting a new partner, as they live in perpetual hope of a reconciliation.

Whatever has bought Betty to this situation, the fact is that she is a depressed woman with few friends. She only talks to me and Julie as neighbours and names my mum as a good friend. We have helped her often when she locks herself out or needs help to contact her daughter. It is a pleasure. She can be a bit of a nightmare, but we all laugh about it as being the way she typically goes about her life. Betty is a character, and one always wonders what she will get up to next. Months pass without us seeing her, when she takes to her bed with depression.

For Betty to be knocking on my door to talk to my mum is a first, and we later find out she has new drugs from the doctor for her depression. I suppose they are uppers. She is definitely upbeat, staying here for two hours and wanting to book a holiday with my mum for late summer. It seems that the drugs are effective. Today is freezing, and after she leaves, we see Betty from our window, in just her thin cardigan, chatting to the builder who is working on repairing her front steps across the road from us. My mum mentions how cold it is and that she should go inside. All of a sudden, my mum exclaims, "She's fallen over!" as she watches from our kitchen window. I look over the road to see Betty, marooned, kneeling, facing up her steps in just her socks, unable to move. It turns out that she has stood in wet concrete in her slippers and turned to walk away without realising, thus falling and leaving her slippers embedded in the concrete. The builder is pretending he has not seen what happened, busying himself. Bill, in his eighties, has rushed out to rescue her by first helping her to her feet and then unearthing her slippers from the concrete. I have to say it was quite the funniest thing I have ever seen in my life. I know it sounds cruel, but if you knew Betty, you would understand. Nobody was hurt, and I don't think anyone has actually ever died of embarrassment. If it were possible, there would have been carnage on those steps.

I know these moments are depicted in television comedy sketches and in cartoons, but that is the first time I have ever witnessed in real life such perfect comedic timing. It's so much better when it happens live. I am giggling a little even now. We did see Betty actively mooching about later that day. She is fine. Whatever next? I can't help but think that these drugs rev up the mind and the aging body can't keep up. The excited mind makes promises that the aging body can't keep. The resulting comedy is okay as long as nobody gets hurt. I am sure Betty would accept the risk for the improvement in her mood generally, living her life rather than sleeping it away. I suppose she will eventually develop a tolerance for the drugs and either need some time off before resuming or some new drugs. Who would have thought that as a recipe for comedy all you really need are some antidepressants and some wet cement? Mix them together and wait.

Time Waits for Nobody

Recently my mum and my sister drove past my uncle's house, which had been decorated and sold after his recent death. He had lived there since 1954. My sister was upset because it was obvious that selling the house and sharing the money out had been an urgent task amongst his family, and it all seemed so final. I feel that life rolls on, not stopping for anyone. We wouldn't want it any other way. Even though we may hate the way life is heading, it must always head in one direction or another, determined by our choices. The richness is in our personal memories, those small moments.

I recall a story my mum told me recently about when she lived in Ireland with my dad. A bird, a wren, had flown into the house, and my dad walked up to it gently and held out his finger. The wren hopped onto Dad's finger, and he took it outside to freedom. However, the bird did not want to leave, and finally he had to encourage it to fly away. This was not the dad that I had known at all. Mum retold many similar such tales, which she had never talked about previously. That personal memory that mum shared is priceless and makes me remember my dad differently. She described him being authentically as he really was, and not in the role that he played for me, his son, as my teacher and authority figure. I am happy to get to know the real man, even belatedly, and honoured and a little saddened that he took his role as father so seriously as to never show his true self.

This would be considered quite a sacrifice in a time when parents want to be their kids' best friends above all else. Maybe that is why society is lacking values. More parenting and less best-buddy is needed. The respect comes belatedly, but it will surely come. Knowing my real dad explains much of why I am who I am. I wonder whether my kids know me. Maybe they do a little more than I knew my dad but not the total package. Maybe that is something that they will take on board as they mature and reflect more on life. Many of life's lessons are always present; they just await the readiness of the student to see the truth. I have made a conscious effort to be more real than my dad was for me for my kids and will continue to do so.

The great worry for me is that students (everyone) will spend their whole lives distracted by stuff and never live to be aware and reflect upon the great lessons that surround them. These lessons will be there for them when they awaken to what is genuinely important and less than the window dressing of life that has occupied them up to this point. I bless the day that I was forcibly awakened. My suffering led me to different choices. I would make no more choices for others or for what others might think, whoever those others might be. No more choosing the norm. My choices would be my own for the first time ever in my life.

My life is not "normal". The people that I care about accept that choice totally, and new friends have appeared who have similar beliefs or are ready to question the accepted behaviours and beliefs for themselves. You can't be an individual and the same as somebody else. Search out those lessons, and keep searching for the rest of your life. The pressure to live a normal life, the same life as others, is constant and unforgiving. Good luck.

 Ambushed

It was a Saturday, and there was to be a big soccer match in the town, between two teams that historically have a reputation for violence. The town was full of police and riot squads from an early hour. However, I was to experience violence from a most unexpected situation. We were walking through the town centre in order to time how long it would take Julie to walk to catch a bus on the following Monday morning. As we walked through a small industrial area, we noted that some gypsies or travellers (just a name) had set up camp in the small side road. We just continued chatting and walking as if to pass through their camp. There were children playing in the road. Two men were cleaning a van, and the lady of the camp seemed to be sorting her washing out. As we passed, a little boy, about five or six years old I would guess, the smallest amongst them although a little rotund, shouted and threw a thick slice of buttered bread at me, aiming to get it down inside my jacket. He thought he had succeeded, although he had just splattered my jacket with butter as the bread hit me and fell to the ground. He ran alongside me in a victory dance, screaming to his darling little friends who were not quite as brave.

45

There was a brief moment when I could have strangled him, but I quickly saw the funny side of the boy's wild behaviour. I was reminded of a time when my father drove me through the Dublin docks area when I was young and the car was chased and pelted with sticks and stones by what can only be described as wild children. There are groups of the community that fall just on the edge or outside of real law and order through disregard for the education system and the general laws of the land. I discuss social control very much. I do have a problem with social control and the subtle conditioning of humans to obey at the cost of any real freedom in life. However, at this time and by this event, I am reminded of the need for controlling the masses. This young man was no automaton. If all of society behaved this way, we would indeed have some major problems – at least a bread and butter shortage!

I would say my problem with social control comes into play when individual cases are not considered, when common sense takes a back seat. Many people can indeed create their own values and be good even though some of their behaviours may fall outside of the law. An example would be drug use by certain consenting adults, such as Huxley and Freud, that would take them outside of the law but nobody could dispute their contribution to society. I am sure there are many such cases of intelligent people creating their own values to live by that would take them outside of both the norms and society's laws. One has to know the laws in order to break them. Many of you reading this now will fall into the category of breaking laws that you feel are of no use to you as ethical beings. Nietzsche would be proud.

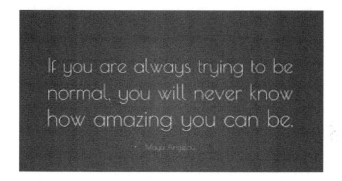

Social control also is used by profit-mongers in order to manipulate more control over consumers with erroneous beliefs or with conditioned responses that are hardly ever questioned. A perfect example of this would be my old favourite, mobile phones. When prisoners are freed, they are often tagged so they can be located. Is one's mobile phone not a very expensive tag amongst many others, such as one's computer? Ask yourself this question: Does anybody have privacy in the twenty-first century? I think we would be extremely offended if we knew the true extent of the personal information held on any one of us. Conspiracy theory? That is the way governments trivialise comments such as this. What better way of covering up than by creating an indifference and complacency about any issue? Treat it as a joke; then people will laugh with us and drop the subject. We all have friends who use this tactic. They use humour to protect themselves from any subject that may make them uncomfortable. It would seem to work effectively, all the way from the most insecure school clown to the highest government officials. Such officials are, however, just as much a part of the social-control machine as we all may be. The accusation of conspiracy theories is a manipulative ruler's way of making light when they are threatened by the truth.

 Crap

As a lifetime dog owner, I am finding some dog owners' behaviour a little perplexing. People talk about responsible dog owners, but I think there are as many irresponsible dog owners as there are irresponsible people generally in society, which is too many. I am not convinced that owning a dog makes you more likely to act

Would you decorate your tree like this?

Please bin the bags

www.cornwall.gov.uk
Telephone: 0300 1234 212

CORNWALL
COUNCIL

responsibly than the average non-dog owning citizen. This is not the root of my confusion. Here is my question. Why does a person go to all of the trouble of scooping up dog poop and putting it in bag and then throwing the poop-containing bag up the nearest tree? How is a tree full of a variety of bags of poop any kinder to our environment? I noticed I have a poop bag in my apple tree in the garden, obviously launched from the waste ground at the back of my house. My first thought was that it may be a protest against there not being enough waste bins provided for the disposal of poop. But I have seen the infamous poop trees very close to waste bins. One can't expect to find bins along every inch of a dog-walking route. That is just ridiculous; one might just as well install doggy toilets.

I have no clue as to why anyone would launch poop up a tree after scooping it into a bag. Maybe the feel of poop in the bottom of a carrier bag gives one the uncontrollable urge to swing into action and become a poop thrower. Will poop-throwing ever make the Olympics? I doubt it very much. Why do you think they do it? I would just add here that any non-dog owners who may be feeling smug and superior need only take a look at the litter, human spittle, and half-eaten food along the paths and sidewalks to bring them back to earth with a bump. I have so often witnessed the worst littering right next to waste bins. At times I do wonder if there is really any hope for the human race, when many of them don't even care enough about the planet which is their home or about others in their society to put rubbish in a bin.

I will use "they" to describe a very small percentage of the population that litters or lets their dogs mess the public highways. As I have yet to find anyone that actually admits to not using the bins provided. Once confronted we all become perfectly behaved citizens. The rubbish is always from junk-food establishments; could we argue that people who eat junk food are equally irresponsible with their other behaviours? Are junk-food junkies antisocial, greedy, and self-serving? They would not be alone, as it could also be argued that I have just described our society under the power of capitalism. Often what we complain about the most is something that we may be guilty of personally. The truth is that "they" just don't care enough about anything to change, unless it is to accumulate more stuff. "They" exist to have. Here's my simple request to that small percentage: Please put your rubbish and poop in a bin. I have made it sound as if I live in a litter and poop infested area. I am just focusing on it at the moment. It will not seem as bad when I shift my focus elsewhere. It does need to improve.

Laws of Convenience

Many years ago when I was young – many years ago – double-parking was a traffic offence. By double-parking, I mean parking directly opposite another car in such a way as to reduce the width of the road. I assume for it to be considered an offence it was thought to be a dangerous practice. Funny, then, how it is no longer considered dangerous, together with many other obviously dangerous parking practices. I wonder whether this has anything to do with the greed of making and selling more cars for profit trumping any safety issue? That may indicate that the law is more about bringing in revenue, collected for alleged offences rather than any actual real offences. Is this another indicator of the greed of mankind ruling his every move? So now there are cars lined both sides of the road, like two solid walls separating one side from the other. That's just what we need, yet more walls and barriers between us.

Gone are the days when children could play in the streets and neighbours walked and talked up and down the roads, able to see each other unimpeded by abandoned lumps of metal and unthreatened by speeding traffic. To make matters yet more dangerous, motorists now park actually up on the pavement or sidewalk. At times they totally block the way, often pulling onto the sidewalk or pavements while pedestrians are walking in that area or moving off while there is the danger of colliding with flesh and blood and startling the pedestrians.

Cars bring out the worst side of human beings – and that is normal car-driving behaviour! Cars seem to take priority over people. Machines rule the roads and the pedestrian routes to the extent that many drivers do not even have the common decency to stop at pedestrian crossings any longer. Car owners and drivers feel they are more important than pedestrians. If they do stop or slow down, it is at their discretion, as if they are doing the poor pedestrians a favour! I was under the assumption that to stop at pedestrian crossings is the law. But it's yet another law that is conveniently ignored by the authorities, such as parking on the pavement. As a full-time pedestrian, I frequently have to walk in the road in order to continue on my journey. I am reasonably mobile; heaven knows how the less mobile or mothers with pushchairs manage to get anywhere in a safe manner. Progress? It just doesn't sound like a step forward but rather a step backwards, adding to the regression of a human society that is blissfully unaware that their lives are becoming increasingly dependent on, and controlled by, machines. And they are paying for the privilege. But how high will the price ultimately prove to be for the coming generations?

> Trust me...
> You're not as good
> at texting while driving
> as you think you are.
>
> -The driver behind you

 Gravity-Defying Grandma

You are aware by now that Julie has been cycling as part of our new life philosophy of rejecting as much technology as we can in favour of more planet-friendly habits. There are many hills in our part of the world, and for months Julie has been trying to pedal all the way to the top of one particularly long ascent. One day she made it and was jumping about and enthusing about the achievement the moment she arrived home and every day since. She was even commenting on how easy it was and how she absolutely flew up there every night now.

However, lest we all start to look for her name added to the British successes at the Tour de France, we should take stock for a second. A week after her victory, in a moment of brutal honesty, she confided in me that that very day she had been overtaken by the pounding hooves of two joggers. She did mention that they must surely be professionals, as they were as swift as the wind. I think that moment placed a little bit of perspective on the speed of Julie's ascent. Having said that, I very much doubt – no, I am sure I would not be able to pedal up that hill all the way from bottom to top. Julie is now talking about possibly trying the next-higher gear in the near future. This is a perfect example of small goals to reach a larger target. I am not sure whether she plans to take on any joggers. Maybe not professionals to start, and preferably joggers that are unaware they are in a race to the top of the hill.

 Pee, Potatoes, and Premature Ejaculation

I have a challenge for all those powerful brains out there that feel they have great control over their human tools, the tools gifted by evolution and nature. Are you feeling you have mastered most that life can throw your way? Why is it that the same person can love boiled potatoes and mashed potatoes but heaven forbid they find a lump in their mashed potatoes? It would seem that the disastrous situation of lumps in the mashed potatoes is impossible for the human brain to cope with. Another life trial that seems to test even the most Zen of us is needing to use the toilet and having to wait for quite a long while. Humans may be able to meditate for hours but don't seem to be able to distract themselves long enough not to pee their pants. It can be done. Sorry for anyone with a medical complaint; you are not included in this.

Take your mind away from the toilet situation and you may even forget you wanted to go. It's the opposite of mindfulness. I think it is a great challenge when I am consumed by the feeling and have miles to walk before I can find relief. I usually start to have a one-way conversation with the dogs. I normally chat to Smudge, as Jake has a look that makes me feel that I'm insane and seems to need bribing with treats to even think about listening. I am insane, but I can do without the reminder from a twelve inch-high terrier. Smudge wags her tail, and I can pretend she understands as I dance, just a little cross-legged, down the road. The dancing stops when I finally manage to forget I had been busting for a pee. The practice can be quite uncomfortable, though, and possibly a little wet until you master your new skill. For the gents, I bet premature ejaculation could be cured the same way, although thinking about

something unrelated to your partner or sex while you are making love may not go down too well. Your partner will know by your vacant look and sudden apparent attempt not to be present. Poor timing can be messy, not to mention a little embarrassing.

 ## Picture-Postcard Snow

My mum has recently moved out of our town to a village quite close by. For some reason she feels that she will be having totally different weather conditions than we do. She often texts me telling me the weather they are having, when we are experiencing exactly the same about six miles away. I joke with her and tell her when she is having picture-postcard snow that we only get the crappy snow in our town. It's much like respect when you travel; it only comes if you pay for it. Picture-postcard snow only turns up in affluent areas. She always used to do this when she lived in Cornwall and Ireland. She needs to know that her weather conditions are better than ours or worse than ours, whatever will give them the edge in importance in her mind. A sort of weather one-upmanship. Whatever you get, we get better, worse, longer, and harder. She knows I gave up letting the weather do anything but uplift me many years ago when I realised I was never able to change it. I love all weather. I love my mum thinking she gets special weather. The English really are obsessed with the weather, if my mum is any gauge. Maybe if we pay more rates or poll tax we will stop getting the crappy snow and get some picture-postcard, grade A, whiter-than-white snow. The social climbers get all the best weather. The picture is Julie and two of our pups at the local park.

 Pondering Perfection Again

It's 6.30 a.m., and I am off to the woods on this mild, windless, dark and wet morning. Smudge, as usual, is a little reluctant in the rain until she gets used to the idea. She hates being showered also and sulks for most of the day if anyone other than me attempts to wash her. She seems to forgive me quite quickly, probably because I chat to her all the time I am washing her.

The light doesn't really break through the dark curtain much before 7.30 a.m. amazingly, the entire woods seems to be made up of silhouettes; even the dogs are in silhouette. I must be in silhouette also for anyone looking. There are no colours, as they seem to arrive with the light; there are just dark shapes. The light will bring the colours, and even though we had a full moon last night, there seem to be no chinks in nightfall's armoured curtain. I begin to ponder once more on the concept of perfection and what that actually means.

For any person striving for perfection, it is elusive and unattainable, as perfection is ever-changing. For the body, the media and profit-mongers would have us believe perfect women are thin with big boobs, perfect hair, and rows of white teeth – hopefully the right amount, but who knows these days? Maybe they just put in as many as are needed to fill up the space and then add an extra one for luck. For men, the ideal is perfect hair, chiselled midsection, square jaw, a perfect mouthful of pearly white gnashers, and lots of muscles. Perfection is simply unattainable; we all know that perfect people have surgery to change. Does that mean that they weren't perfect in the first place? Perfection will be something different tomorrow. Is perfect an illusion, and does it have to be the same for all? We are all born perfectly unique and seem to have forgotten how to love ourselves. Have we allowed the out-of control consumption machine to convince us that we should look different or that to be perfect we must spend money and consume their products? Maybe we need to love and accept our God-given perfection and not try to meet others' ideas of what we should be so that somebody along the line can make a profit changing us. We should all laugh at fake perfection and see it for the joke that it really is. That would be a good place to start.

The search for perfection certainly does not result in peace of mind. I wonder if perfect peace of mind would be a more realistic aim. Peace of mind will be discovered inside of yourself, not anywhere on the outside. It comes with the acceptance that life is good and you are a good person (most of the time) doing the best you can with what you know at this time. You look after your health, keep fit, and balance all areas of your life in a calm manner. Most issues that we are conditioned to overreact about, such as the weather, we can turn around and smile about with very little effort. If the constant sale of perfection is hounding you, just eliminate it from your life. Don't read the magazines or watch the television programmes that attempt to sell you happiness by changing you or by selling you more stuff to make you more happy or happy all the time. It won't work, and you will waste your money and end up disappointed. Start to look inside, and you might just be surprised at how inexpensive a little peace of mind can be. Spend your life getting better and getting to know yourself. You may even discover an authentic original that doesn't exist for others, public opinion, and a life of consumption for our capitalist society. Happy hunting.

One-Dimensional Planet

In conversation with my sister, I remarked how disconnected from nature and the planet people had become. She excitedly jumped in, pointing out that on her journey to work in the car she took the country lanes and saw a whole list of wildlife. She really believed that viewing wildlife from her metal box with the radio on, and watching the occasional David Attenborough special on the goggle box, connected her to the planet. I bet she is not alone in that assumption. Maybe she is even giving to animal charities now and again.

My opinion is that nature can't be experienced unless you are using all of your senses and have dispensed with all technology and gadgets for the experience. That means no car, no phone, and no music players. Nature has depth and cannot be experienced through a flat-screen goggle box or a window. Nature has sounds and smells; it must be touched and felt. As great as it is to watch the wind in the trees on a stormy day from a car or window, the experience will never come close to actually being out in the wind and rain, feeling, hearing, seeing, and smelling the storm as you walk. The same can be said of any weather condition or nature opportunity. Your resistance to this thought is a measure of your disconnection with the natural world. Try it. Get outside and leave the twenty-first century behind. Just live it. Otherwise nature is just another picture of scenery. What a waste. Are our expectations too low? Maybe all we need is some great expectations for nature to make even greater every day.

Related to this, I looked out of the window on a snowy Sunday morning and thought it odd to see bare human footprints in our driveway. Upon further investigation, I discovered that Julie had wanted to feel the snow on her feet the night before so had gone out to the bins in her bare feet – just living it! She said it felt good.

Lost Childhood

I noticed today that my dogs love children because they are more fun than adults. They exude fun from every pore. They giggle and play and give off a whole different energy than adults or even many adolescents that have been conditioned to become serious by adults and society control. My dogs can hear the uninhibited sounds of children well before they see them and get very excited. The dogs become slightly less easy for me, a serious controlling adult, to control just like the children before conditioning takes its toll and they become socialised, the uninhibited free spirit is reduced and controlled and in some cases lost forever. This reaffirms my belief that we all need to be more childlike.

I was told as a young man that I was too sensible for my age. Why might this be the case? The main reason was the insistence by my Father of certain behaviour standards and my desire to please him at all costs. Starved of any real affection that was as close as I came to any real sign of love existing. I know better now but still fight to keep from taking life too seriously which is my default way of being. Julie is in touch with her inner child and that does help to keep reminding me to lighten up. As I age I am again finding the

fun in life that for many years was only available to me through alcohol or drugs. I lost the ability to laugh for many years. Life was a serious business. I am now able to laugh uncontrollably at all sorts of stuff that tickles my sense of humour. It feels good to regain that childishness that had been buried deep for too many years in my shadow bag. I still have much work to do to make fun Adam my default persona. I will get there; of that I am certain. I will at least get better.

The shadow bag is a term used by poet Robert Bly to describe how, as we grow up and become conditioned we put all of the thoughts, feelings and behaviours that do not suit our development within our culture into our shadow bag. Much of our darker side resides in the bag but also good stuff like uninhibited fun and laughter in my case. Becoming a whole person does depend on reopening our shadow bags and finding the parts of ourselves that can make us whole. Every man and woman is everything and balancing the psyche is the key to wholeness according to Jungian psychology. For example we contain both feminine and masculine, good and bad, pride and humility and the list goes on, and it is the balancing of these opposites that leads to individuation or enlightenment. I will discuss this more further on in this book and future books. It is vital to our progress to know and accept what we contain in our shadows.

I still feel that being too serious is my default setting. But awareness of the issue means that it will change if I work at it. The ideal balance of fun and seriousness can be found. As can the ideal balance of masculine and feminine, good and bad and pride and humility be reached once one is made aware of the imbalance. We contain both opposites and there is a sacred middle ground where we can find peace of mind. Maybe only fleetingly but worth the effort.

I would guess that fun Adam was put in my shadow bag when my Father insisted on the opposite behaviour as my normal behaviour. I think he took his responsibility of parenting more as a job of producing a perfect man devoid of emotions, masculine and good at everything. An object of pride for him as a Father to place before others. I was never a person. I was a possession to be bragged about. The only praise I ever received was hearing him brag to others or being told by my Mother how proud he was (of his possession).

I will start a welcome home fun Adam campaign to integrate him once more into my psyche. My dogs love my sensible, reliable side to feed and house them but find most of their fun elsewhere. They are so well trained because of my sense of discipline. I am the same on myself. They look forward to Julie's return from work for some light hearted fun and games. I am a work in progress as are we all.

Hindsight is a wonderful thing. I was given too much responsibility at a very young age. Much the same as my Father suffered looking after his brothers in Dublin as the oldest brother. My childhood was cut short as was his. I only ever remember my Father smiling on the odd occasion. He had no fun side as far as I was concerned. Those occasions were generally around my sister. My Father had different rules for the upbringing of his daughter. My sister would have a vastly different account of her childhood. This is true to this day, my Mother still favours my sister and her children with both her money and her time. The unfairness is obvious to all but my

Mother, sister and their families. Such is life, I suppose, we all perceive and process our lives via our personality traits and histories, which can make us seem very out of synch with others. That is a sad thing for a son to reflect on, but I do understand that as parents we all do the best we can with what we know at that period in our lives, based mostly on our past experiences. It is one of our purposes in life to transcend our parents in every way possible. Not to emulate them but to rise above the last generation is the task of each and every new generation.

What seems like obvious behaviour to me may not even register with others. I believe my Father wanted to make my life better than the one he experienced as a young man. But he couldn't escape from the conditioning and made many of the same mistakes but with less physical violence. I was to be taught and moulded every moment of my life. I wonder how many parents are guilty of

treating their children as objects to be made perfect in the mind of overzealous parents. Starved of affection as the showing of any emotion is not thought manly. I hope the current generations do not hold these antiquated beliefs. Young people are already perfect and just need some guidance and unconditional love to flourish. Sadly, most love is conditional on something once you look under the surface. I sincerely hope I treat my children with more fairness.

That will be my intention from the lessons I have learned due to my parent's behaviour. Maybe inadvertently they have given me the greatest gift of all. I do not for one second blame my parents as we all behave in the best way we are able from our limited points of view at any given time. We do our best under pressure from the hidden forces that shape our identities and behaviour such as our biological drives, our cultural conditioning and the media onslaught of how to be ideal. The result is anything but ideal. We all have our own unique paths to forge.

I have already made great strides with the huge positive changes I wish to make to my persona (ego). Should you be facing similar issues? The turning point is becoming aware of the inner work one needs to do. Knowing yourself better each day is how to become aware and enables one to strip another layer of pretence from your fake identity. Maybe it's time to make friends with your shadow.

"IT IS NEVER TOO LATE TO HAVE A HAPPY CHILDHOOD" DO SOMETHING CHILDISH... TODAY.

 Beauty And The Beast

In today's society if you are not dreadfully ashamed of your physical self, then you run the risk of being deemed narcissistic. We live in a world where thanks to the media (unrealistic) ideals, the middle way, the balancing of opposites, is never considered when judging others, which is really judging oneself through shadow projection. So next time you are judging another person with strong feelings, investigate what it is about that person that you need to deal with in yourself. If it is just observation then no problem but if the judgement affects you physically and emotionally and unearths strong feelings, then you may want to start searching your shadow bag for clues. The judgement is on yourself. This is an amazing way to get to know yourself on a much deeper level and to uncover your shadow.

 Decent Exposure

We are exposed daily to all kinds of information which needs little or no effort on our part. This information is fed to us for two main reasons, to make somebody a profit and for reasons of social control. We are being exploited for our money and obedience and subtly told what to think so we think they are our own thoughts. I call this type of drip fed conditioning information "indecent exposure", we are bombarded constantly with this type. The other type of exposure, the good type, the progressive type I call "decent exposure". We have to make an effort to discover the situations and the knowledge that is not the norm for us. Reading books to test us away from the easily found crap and getting into situations out of our comfort zones. Becoming curious and exposing ourselves to opposing thoughts and opinions to the ones we hold and identify with so vehemently. Taking our existing thoughts and beliefs and turning them on their heads. Doing something we never do like riding a bike or even walking, taking a different route or eating a different food. If religion scares us, read a well-balanced book on the subject, such as those by Karen Armstrong. If we are religious, then study all of the other religions to better understand the good and bad in all religions. I read about all religions and it is scary how ignorant many confirmed orthodox religious folk are about their own religion. Particularly those that knock on your door to sell their ideas. Once challenged to an open-minded discussion they are as robotic babes.

The spirit of progress here is to expose yourself to people, situations and knowledge away from the norms. Be curious and liken it to a treasure hunt in which the precious moments and amazing insights are the reward. Trust me when I say that the search is totally worth the effort.

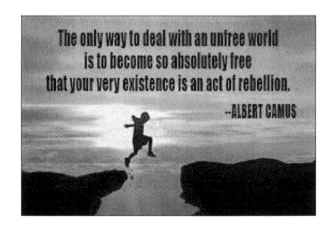

The only way to deal with an unfree world is to become so absolutely free that your very existence is an act of rebellion.

--ALBERT CAMUS

Earliest Memories

My personality type or typology as it is called, is an introverted, intuitive feeler/thinking. Or at least that is my tendency. My thinking and feeling are very even. At least that is what I have decided. The important thing to note is that I am an introvert. Julie is an extravert. These traits are thought to be the least likely part of one's psyche to change. Hence the ploys and roles we play in order to hide our true personalities. The first half of life is not a good place for introverts and it easy to see why I thought that developing, through lifting weights, a muscular body as a coat of armour against all of the perceived threats was a good idea. It doesn't work. It is the inside that needs to be trained. I like to be alone. I like to think and reflect and I am uncomfortable in some of the most unlikely situations. I will not even go to the bar for drinks in a pub for feeling exposed. I have managed to become quite adept at covering my introversion. Julie is the opposite, so that works well. In actual fact, Julie is the opposite of me in many ways, which is probably why we are together. Or to be more accurate, why our subconscious minds found each other. We complete each other's psyche. And all human beings long to be whole. Which is probably why opposites do attract. The problem is that one needs to be whole without outside help or dependency on others. But that is another problem. I want to give the reader an idea of Julie and I's personalities in order to illustrate what I think is a quite an amazing discovery. I get quite excited about this kind of stuff.

For the last couple of years Julie, when asked how happy she is on a scale of 1 - 10 says 11. I didn't get that at all until I discovered her typology. In my world that is impossible. Julie is very optimistic all of the time or a large part of the time. I am pessimistic and optimistic. I am learning optimism. I am not pessimistic compared to the norm as I have found society frighteningly pessimistic. However, pessimism seems to be my default setting, which I have learned to turn around very quickly through learned optimism techniques. I have to work very hard to look on the bright side 24/7. That is Julie's default setting. Julie's worldview is optimistic. If she ever has moments of pessimism I stare in amazement but it never lasts very long before she has turned herself around again. It usually happens when another pessimist is venting and she gets hooked into the grumpy vibe. Pessimism is very contagious. My worldview is improving but my glass can be half empty very easily. I have developed a persona to facilitate an introvert's survival in an extravert's world. I expect the worse, I can spot trouble a mile away. That is because I am on the lookout for trouble. I analyse every situation and am overly cautious. I would make a great health and safety officer (Actually my types recommended vocations are creative writing and counsellor, both of which are part of my chosen world, all good there). I expect people to think the worse of me. Julie is the opposite. Julie is part of my survival kit. Not very romantic but that is probably why I needed Julie in my life at the outset without ever realising what my psyche was doing, I was strengthening its position or covering the areas that it couldn't cover. Our subconscious minds run our lives for us until we wake up and join the subconscious in co-creating our existence as one mind. That is if we can master our minds and the universe to the point of knowing how it might work. A constant learning and flowing process. Never fixed. I am suspicious minded. I hasten to add all of these traits are what I work on daily and most have changed because I have worked to understand and change them. This description is my persona left to its own devices, without any choice from me.

Okay, now I feel you know Julie and me a little better. What was the point? I was reading Scott Peck's book, The Road Less Travelled recently. In the book I latched onto a passing comment that it is precisely our earliest childhood memory that determines our worldview as adults. I had heard this before but for some reason it became relevant right now. I instantly remembered mine. It is etched in my psyche. I was dumbfounded how accurate the theory seemed to be in relation to my development and my worldview.

My earliest childhood memory was at the age of between my learning to walk and four years old. I can't really narrow it down more than that. It is not important. What is important is that I was totally dependent on my Mother for my safety and security. We were outside the house we were living in at that time and going shopping or such like. I would have been holding my Mother's hand. I can't help but wonder if she let go of my hand to protect herself. A natural reaction for a girl that was only young herself, in her early twenties. I do know that nobody was holding my hand when I met my fate. I do not hold my Mother responsible for it but I do think that young parents in general are not ready for parenting. I am sure Julie and I messed up more often than we would like to admit. It is also quite frightening how a seemingly innocuous event such as the one I will describe next can have such a traumatic impact on a young person's life. And each and every one of us will have similar events that have impacted who we are and how we view the world and our place in that world. Our worldview. The responsibility of parenting becomes a sobering thought and a challenging task when looked at in any depth and considering the child's developing psyche on top of everything else entailed in being a parent.

The event.

I am only aware because of this memory, that we had a teenage downs syndrome girl living next door. I have no recollection of her either before or after this event. To me at this time she was huge. This day she came running down her path and pushed me over, hurting me quite badly. I remember the event as if in slow motion, and I have a vivid memory of the grey gravel that had to be painstakingly plucked out of knees. I suppose she was excited to see us and this was her way of showing it. The upshot of this story is that in my very small world I was physically attacked for no reason that I could find acceptable in my infant world. At the time I was entrusted to the person supposed to provide protection. I am assuming that up to this point the protection had been good. This would have been a severe shock to my system, in what had been a very comfortable world for me. I was very safe and secure. Another early memory is being lost and alone in the town centre and the feeling of blind panic that ensued. With these recollections I remember both being abandoned and overwhelmed, arguably the root causes of all of our future metal issues. I think being an introvert only makes each situation worse.

After such a traumatic experience it is no surprise that my worldview is that the world is a dangerous place and that you can't trust any person to protect you. I prefer to be isolated and hate large groups and crowds. I am unsure as to whether your experiences shape your personality type or not, but my introversion was either the result of my memory or an incident that an introvert would not relish. My other childhood memories are of me playing alone with my toys. My Mother used to say that I was as good as gold just getting on with playing on my own. I guess I was just glad not to be taken out into the warzone unprotected and unarmed as that was my memory of the outside world. I seemed to retire into my own little world at that time. Strangely my favourite toys were soldiers, forts, cowboys and Indians. Maybe I was developing my warlike shadow side. I remember the play very well. One of only a few memories I retain from my childhood. I have over the years managed to develop coping mechanisms to overcome my understandably distorted world view.

That's (more than) enough about me.

Now this is where it gets good.

Julie's earliest childhood memory?

11/10 happy Julie remembers with fondness being an angel in the pre-school nativity play. So while I was being physically assaulted Julie was living every little girl's dream. Right up there in importance with being a princess.

Enough said. Julie's worldview matches this memory perfectly. It blows my mind how accurate this is. Our earliest experience telling us so much about ourselves.

My worldview was one based on fear. A worldview that I have changed beyond recognition and will continue to work on until I am an angel also. Luckily I found a flesh and blood guardian angel to help me along the way. There is a certain romance about that. I see that now. It has been a long road and it is getting more interesting with the passing of time and the gaining of wisdom. The task now is to take on the traits of the other to become as close to whole as is possible unaided. That is the goal for each of us. Independent wholeness.

What leads us to remember these memories is the impact they have had, and are continuing to have one way or another on our lives. Otherwise we would remember everything. We remember the stuff that has shaped our lives for better or worse. These memories are a rich source of material for any of us wanting to get better and needing to understand ourselves for personal and spiritual growth. Adversity is where we find the most growth in life.

Would the world be a better, more optimistic place if everybody's earliest memories were happy ones? Perhaps, but all we can do is work to create significantly more happy memories than unhappy ones. That is quite a noble purpose in life. But we might then lose many valuable learning experiences. I still think it is worth the endeavour whilst making sure we acknowledge our shadow side. As a repressed shadow is a dangerous thing and will find a way not to be ignored.

 The Power Of Influence

Parents affect their children's outlook in life so much. Some bad habits are so ingrained in families that the children don't stand a chance of choosing for themselves. The choices already having been made by the examples being set. Are we letting our indifference to health and fitness affect those around us, particularly the ones we love? This role really is so important. We all influence our nearest and dearest silently all the time with our memes, this is not a role we can decide we don't want. Memes are the mimicked behaviour, the transferring of ideas, beliefs and attitudes to others and it all takes place mentally and silently. Memes pass from mind to mind via hundreds of thousands of imitations, they are not necessarily good or bad; they simply spread easily. Memes impact our behaviour throughout our lives and can influence our habits if we don't realise and change those ingrained beliefs that are not serving us well. Are we sending out the right messages? Could our children, friends, parents or neighbours be setting us the right example? Are we setting them the right example? Do we take our position as role models seriously? Do we even realise that we are all role models? Just because we are older does that mean we cannot learn from our children? We have a lifetime of bad and some good habits just waiting to be passed on to our friends, children and even neighbours. When is the right time to take our role model status seriously? Does the fact that the results are not immediately obvious like they would be with bad behaviour or poor manners mean that we ignore our responsibilities? Whether we realise the consequences of the example we set or not, there are, and will always be people that love us and look to us for a lead in life. We influence others and that is a fact. We all make mistakes and none of us are perfect but there has to be a time when we look to set or follow examples of others with habits that will set up our families for generations by actually changing the activity culture. Are we teaching our kids by example, to eat, drink and sit around doing nothing or play computer games? Is our fear of exercise influencing our children, significant others or any person that spends time in our company on a regular basis? Do you think walking is for people that don't have cars or can't drive? We can all make good or better health and fitness habits part of our culture permanently by starting the ball rolling with small changes here and now.

If you are overweight, unfit and sedentary and every social occasion for you involves food and drink, if your idea of relaxing is watching television or playing computer games, then you are following an example that could lead to a miserable life and an early grave. You are also setting this behaviour as normal and making it part of your culture to be handed down to future generations via your memes. In effect this behaviour has become part of your legacy. I know this may sound harsh but that is the whole point, our lifestyles make us miserable and are killing us and we do nothing but joke about it until it is too late. Obesity is no laughing matter. Heart attacks are not funny. Bad habits lead to misery sooner or later is that what we want for ourselves and for our families? To stress this even more our influence and roles as mentors is preordained whether we like it or not that is how society habits are reinforced. And no longer can our ingrained habits be dismissed as not harming anyone but ourselves that is simply not true and just plain irresponsible. Overnight with these discoveries we have become aware that we are even more responsible and closer bonded to all of humanity. Just for a second as you sit there ask yourself this question. Discounting your wise words, and we all have plenty of them, what messages are you sending out with your lifestyle and your behaviour? Do you live a do as I say not as I do existence? Are you 100% happy that your message is the one you mean to deliver? Julie and I know that we have much to work on in our lives, but we also thrive in the knowledge that how we behave and our lifestyle can and does make a real difference to people one way or the other. This awareness gives real meaning to our lives that may otherwise have gone unnoticed. This influence is less about loud words than good deeds, habits and behaviours that will silently flow from mind to mind and become learned behaviours. A point worth considering here also is that while we are thinking about our influence on others we ourselves are constantly under attack by mind viruses both good, bad and indifferent. Not to panic but be mindful of what you expose yourself to in the way of negative and sensationalised bad news, violence and advertising. These mediums can weaken even the strongest resolve. On the flip side be receptive to good news, nature and all things positive and you will set yourself up to lead by example. You can ensure you are back in control and not being brainwashed and conditioned by an often complaining and selfish society or businesses wanting you to use their unhealthy products for the sole purpose of increasing their profits.

 ## Disposable Life

Gaia is the earth viewed as a vast self-regulating organism. For me this would extend to all life on earth. There are, I believe, various incidents that could offer proof that earth does in fact operate within a certain balance and a small change in one aspect always results in a change in the totality. An instance would be the extinction of one life form affecting others, causing at times, a catastrophic domino effect. Resulting in the loss of other species that were dependant in one way or another on the first extinction. Obviously most human beings are too arrogant and self-serving to even care most of the time. Believing the planet is the property of the human race to do with as we please. Usually for profit, and holding the belief that more is better. For the sake of this article let us say that earth is indeed a self-regulating organism (Gaia). The first point would be that the millions spent on finding another planet habitable for humans would be a total waste as we are one with this planet and our futures are eternally linked for better or worse. So it would seem that we are trashing our home with no place else to live. So the word would be harmony in all things and in our relationships with others enjoying the same life experience from their own unique perspective.

This leads me to the question - Has everything in life become throw-away to the point that when life gets too difficult, or more realistically, is about to get interesting, we search for a readymade easier option, that we believe is waiting for us rather than learn and grow in our situation, in short has it become easier to trade in everything in our lives when the going gets tough?

 I wonder at whether the people included in our lives are all part of life's challenge that we too often fail at meeting for the promise of something better, something perfect. If we were courageous enough to accept the challenge we would grow and develop as individuals and dig deeper into a human relationship, finding the treasures buried deep within. Too often we find excuses, apportion blame and flee searching for perfection or soul mates that we are taught to believe are waiting tailor-made for our search and collection. Could it be that the secret of making your own perfection is the intended solution and in the process learning to understand, forgive and ultimately experience love and life as the good life should be lived? This would not be in endless happiness but more experiencing the full range of human emotions needed to live a full meaningful and interesting life. I would argue that this is the reality of human experience and that the perfection many strive to find is an imaginary commodity used by capitalist society to tempt us for profit. Many humans are chasing a fairy tale ideal life, lived by perfectly formed photo shopped cyborgs that vaguely resemble the look of a human. Just watch the advertisements on the television what are they selling? Is it a car you are buying or the promise of a better life that supposedly comes with the car. Or are you attempting to emulate the look of a computer generated person in a magazine or on the television.

Stalemate

An industry representative honestly stated that 100% of images are retouched in some way or another. Look very closely and don't show respect to any industry that is fooling you so readily. As an example of a pet hate of mine - Americans, (followed quickly by the rest of the world) spend their time and money faking their whole identity particularly their teeth. And then have the bare faced cheek to ridicule any race, including the British that have chosen to hang on to the teeth they started with. Sadly, the British are now showing signs of following the Americans into that same sad fake smile and Botox era. We are now seeing expressionless faces with rows of white teeth appearing all over Britain. Are teeth even supposed to be white? Or is it just another road to profit, another way to boost the economy? I for one still value the mature grumpy looking face that explodes with personality when breaking into a not so toothy smile. I have noted that the one thing guaranteed to naturally take years off your appearance is to SMILE!!!

The same can be said for love. Individuals search frantically for the ideal love sold to us at every turn. But think on this - which couple are in love the ones kissing and holding hands or the pair arguing on the other side of the road? The answer is both are contained in a loving relationship in reality. Every love has its demonic side. As much as only one side is reported and sold to give an unrealistic picture. True lovers experience the passion of both sides and accept and grow together. A love can never be authentic until the demonic is accepted. Many flit from one relationship to another looking for just the one fluffy side and never ever find it. Accepting your own human demonic and your partners is essential for lasting love. I am however not talking about brutality, that is another subject altogether.

Others search for hidden meaning, confused by global media and advertising, this can never be sustained. Moving from person to person and situation to situation the way they move from product to product or house to house. Never discovering that they themselves are the creators of meaning and that meaning can only be found inside, nothing external can provide the peace of mind we all desire. Every life experience whether considered good or bad moves us closer to the only worthy goal in life. To live that same life to the full with compassion, wisdom, dignity and with peace of mind. This entails accepting the responsibility to make your own life with the hand that your place in history deals you. You will not find a readymade life that you can then be full of blame, excuses and regret about when things don't work out. It is a tragedy to waste a life searching for what you have always had inside of you. Or living your life for others, for material gain or status. Your stuff can never define who you are. Your mistakes do not define you though they may reveal who you are or at least set you on the right track. A lifetime of growth, a lifetime of becoming. Human life is an evolving process, never fixed, ever changing, a different you each and every moment.

 Stuff Peddlers – The Illusion Of Lack.

In a time when we are just starting to be made aware that constant desire, dreams and hopes for that elusive better life are no more than illusory and just serve to make us dissatisfied with our current situation whatever it may be. It would seem that change may not be so easy. It may well be that a lack of something and everything is what keeps human beings moving forward through time. According to existentialist philosophy, a consciousness, a person, can never be completely satisfied. One always interprets every situation in terms of what it lacks for that person. If one is tired, one lacks sleep. If one is hungry, one lacks food. If one is travelling, one lacks being at the destination. The list is seemingly endless. In general, a person always lacks the future to which he is constantly heading. An endless, expectant, march forward in time. Psychologist Alfred Adler believed this is what shaped personality.

It would seem that our capitalist society already knows this and is perfectly happy to take advantage of an innate trait in the human condition in order to make further profits. Producing more and more of what one is immorally hoodwinked and convinced one lacks in order to help the rich get richer and relieve people of their money. I heard another ridiculous example of materialism gone mad earlier. A six-year-old boy being bought an iPad as an educational tool. Who the hell does the parent think they are kidding? An iPad educational? I would like to see any research that could prove an iPad is more educational than say a pen and a journal. Or! Heaven forbid, a book, and this is a big one, read a book. The latter two encourage creativity and free thinking. Even the purchase of the book requires much thought and knowledge about the recipient on the part of the purchaser, be it a parent or a friend. A getting to know them process, if you don't know what to buy then maybe you need to get to know your significant others a bit more. The easy option would be to purchase a chart book, but most of those are popular rubbish. The gift of a journal and a well thought out book, if used and appreciated will be cherished for life. I have just finished To Kill a Mocking Bird. A great read with much to teach any reader. It could be read together for an even richer experience. I have given you your first idea for free. Up to you now to get to know the people you buy for. The iPad just produces another materialistic robot for the future. I would dispute that an iPad's educational purposes would ever overcome the consumption and prospective social networking anti-social problems that will follow the purchase. Whoever convinced the world that social networking sites are good for society could sell ice to Eskimos. Communication is about getting out and meeting people. Not sitting for hours in front of a computer or phone. I am fed up with being in a public place and every person in the vicinity is occupied with their phone. Mums with their toddlers, noses in a phone. That must be great for bonding. How is that developing social skills? The only skill it develops is the vacant grunt, which seems to be the only skill the modern generation have time for. I implore you take some time and teach this new generation the value of stuff that doesn't cost a fortune and teach them the hidden value in the alternatives. The value in personal growth at any age. The value in a book able to reduce grown men to tears with reference to life and the situations that exist in that life once one's head is removed from one's rectum. Once the chains of modern techno distractions are broken. Most of the gadgets pale into insignificance compared to being face to face with real human moments. Passionate about this subject? I think so. We all need to be more concerned with the way our society is heading. And less concerned with buying the next gadget. And yes I am aware of the irony of my posting this on a social networking blog. I am also aware of the dangers of dependency, attachments and addictions related to the modern world. Awareness is the start of awakening and one being in control of the technology as opposed to the technology controlling the human being. Look around and decide which you think is the case in the people you know. The question is can one live without the technology without the belief that it may cause a slow death. I once tried to take a friend's phone from them on a night out as they were constantly using it. The reaction was one of extreme anger and fear. A violent reaction. Enough said. How many of us are addicted to the 21st century one way or the other? Black Friday is another great example. Insanity when viewed from a distance but these people are intelligent human beings such as you and me. These people I am judging are you and me. I am teaching and learning simultaneously.

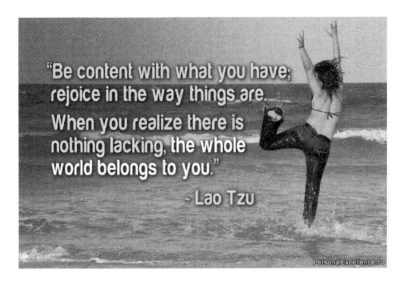

"Be content with what you have; rejoice in the way things are. When you realize there is nothing lacking, the whole world belongs to you."

~ Lao Tzu

PersonalExcellence.co

Next time you feel the need to consume, maybe the real question has to be – Am I really lacking this stuff I feel the need to buy or have I an addiction, an attachment to consuming? The answer will more than likely be that you are dependent on consuming and it has become an attachment that you will now have to fight hard to break free from. This is a war that I constantly fight within myself and I win some battle and lose others. More proof of how we are not as free as we think and may have to fight for our freedom every step of the way. The peddlers of the stuff you are buying know that people attach themselves to consuming and market heartlessly to them accordingly. You are loved by them as long as you have money and the potential to spend it with them. I have looked at consumption in my life and I am attached to certain buying habits. The only way I have found that I can help myself has been to make sure I remove the money from any place too convenient for impulse purchases.

I don't rule out those purchases but we call it "postponing impulses". We buy food and household items and then have twice a year for other purchases. It is surprising how the stuff you will die if you don't own immediately gets forgotten and crossed off the list with the passing of time. Postponing the impulse allows one to make decisions based on rational thinking and not greedy impulses. I have enforced the thinking time on our lifestyle by removing the money and it is the best thing I have ever done. I have removed the issue of that constant "must have" from my life except for two periods a year. I know that is not perfect but it is a start. From living, wanting and buying every moment of your life. The extra peace of mind in knowing that buying is out of the question for most of the year is a priceless feeling. I must say that it was not easy even to make this move. We had a few false starts when we simply had to have stuff for whatever reason we were able to concoct to pacify any ideas to the contrary. But we persevered and the longing for stuff began to lessen and the attachment dropped off to a level where we are back in control as opposed to the peddlers of stuff tempting us to buy and succeeding. If you know yourself well enough and you are prone to over consuming. Then you need to become drastic and remove the money from your convenience. It is just smart to help yourself as much as is possible. Relying on your will power is for losers and it is just another excuse not to stop consuming. The stuff peddlers know you better than you know yourself. You can still have fun with your food and household budget but if it isn't essential you will have to wait until your chosen times to make the purchases. A list that by now you have considered carefully and edited extensively. Our two dates each year are our birthdays. One in April and one I September. Well placed before the summer and the winter. A good time to plan your way into the coming season and make any purchases that will light your way. We effectively take impulse buying out of our lives, not because of any sense of lack but because it is a subtle addiction that we can avoid with aforethought.

It is not a matter of whether one can afford it or not it is about peace of mind and happiness. We buy for the promise of happiness and the feelings we get from wanting stuff. Once we have the stuff we fall flat again. More stuff is not the path to anywhere but having a bigger pile of stuff. Then what? The desire is the addiction. The novelty soon wears off once we have whatever we wanted and a new model (desire) replaces it. It is never ending and great for the profit of the greedy stuff peddlers. If you want to spend your money, then go to see a good psychotherapist, buy some books and learn to be an individual again. It is great to have help in your search for yourself. Start the search for your sacred self. That search begins and ends inside of yourself, there is nothing outside of yourself that will bring you the peace of heart and mind that you are searching for.

Are we really lacking anything in our material worlds? I very much doubt it. Any needs or wants are just levels of greed that we find normal in the 21st century. Our society depends on greed to keep flowing. We are consuming to dress our fake selves. To impress. To find happiness. To be what others expect us to be.

Last time I looked one was unable to purchase awareness, joy or peace of mind. Or the status that we believe is so important and think our stuff will give us, through conspicuous consumption of brands and stuff designed for others to approve of. It even sounds slightly ridiculous that human beings are doing that. Does it really make you more as a person or less to act in this way? "Look at me, look what I have got that I think makes me better than you or at least as good as you, this shows I am somebody important, this gives my life meaning!" The only thing lacking here is any clue of how crazy that behaviour is. It matters not how rich we are; money may even be a hindrance. The real treasures have to be mined inside of yourself. Would great riches improve or wreck the vast majority of people's lives?

Maybe the only thing any of us are lacking is investing the time to reflect on knowing ourselves and being ourselves. And the art of seeing others behind the personas that they have so expensively constructed, if they will only let us glimpse the total humanity that is their sacred self.

 Celebrating Difference

At times I really don't live up to my own standards. When that happens there is always a lesson waiting to show me the right way to act. I don't really believe teaching teaches us much but I do believe we can all actively learn together every single day we are on this planet. My learning takes on many guises and one has to be ready and on the lookout for the messages. Something happened recently that made me stop and think. It doesn't take much to get me thinking these days. Julie and I were out with the dogs at 6am. It is November and the mornings are cold and dark. As we were approaching the local corner shop that isn't on a corner, a gentleman exited wearing just his slippers. A dressing gown (robe) and a smile. He was mumbling to himself and stopped by the waste bin to unwrap a packet of cigarettes he had just purchased. He was obviously in dire need of a cigarette. The dogs, always good judges of people, non-judgemental and free from prejudice ran over to greet him. Julie and I were a little surprised and called the dogs and we each decided independently as we approached that he must live right next to the shop. The manner in which he was dressed to not indicate a longer trip to the shop. We were still obviously uncomfortable. As we walked by we said "Good morning" as the polite (pathetic) thing to do and quickened our pace to regain our comfort zone. Good morning should be a minimum requirement to another human being. Maybe this is an example of English reserve. Behind us we heard the shuffle of his slippers as he followed. We anticipated his entering one of the houses close to the shop. The dogs ran between the shuffling stranger and us. The shuffling was getting faster, as was our pace to elude the stranger, he was obviously trying to catch us. About quarter of a mile from the shop he caught us and asked if we had a light for his cigarette. He was knackered and cold bless him. I noticed he was an elderly gent and that he was making snuffling noises, probably out of breath due to shuffling ever faster for a quarter mile at 6am to catch us up. Our pace did seem to quicken and we didn't speak to each other for an unusually extended period of time. He was probably cold and in places one doesn't normally like to be cold. Apart from the fact that he didn't buy matches while he was in the shop and he was dressed differently for that time of day and that time of year, there really was nothing strange to cause Julie and me to almost run down the road to avoid him. Needless to say I began to analyse the situation the moment he shuffled off down an adjacent road. Hopefully close to home by now. My first conclusion was that the dogs behaved better towards him than we had. Shame being the first emotion. Of our treatment of another human being that may have benefitted from a few friendly words. We weren't rude, rather we were nothing to him. I suppose the fact that he was chasing people down the road in his dressing gown and slippers, for whatever reason, lets us off the hook a little. But these for me are the tests. The precious moments when we grow or lose a little ground to move forward once the lesson has been learned. A reality check for both of us. In hindsight I did think that we may have been the only human contact he would have that entire day. A view that is harsh on us but we didn't acquit ourselves at all well in any case.

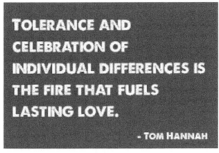

TOLERANCE AND CELEBRATION OF INDIVIDUAL DIFFERENCES IS THE FIRE THAT FUELS LASTING LOVE.

- TOM HANNAH

QuotePixel.com

Are we too intolerant of anybody or any behaviour that is away from the norm? From personal experience, Julie being a physique competitor and a woman and me just being slightly different does create some disgracefully rude behaviour amongst the narrow minded. Maybe it is OK to be cautious but rude and abusive is just unacceptable. This fear, intolerance and lack of understanding of common differences is behind racism, anti-Semitism, sexism, homophobia and prejudice of all kinds. We are aware how wrong it is when dealing with the major issues. However, we are still ignorant of how hurtful it can be to individuals without the power of protection from the law or public opinion. The time has come for us to get back in touch with humanity and realise that behind the exterior that we denigrate so much there is a human being with feelings just like us. They are more the same than different. Compassion is needed.

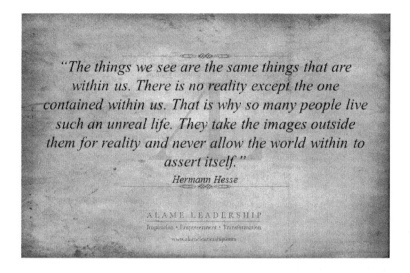

"*The things we see are the same things that are within us. There is no reality except the one contained within us. That is why so many people live such an unreal life. They take the images outside them for reality and never allow the world within to assert itself.*"

Hermann Hesse

ALAME LEADERSHIP
Inspiration • Empowerment • Transformation
www.alameleadership.com

I for one will look out for my elderly gentleman friend and exchange words in a civilised human way. Maybe even hear his story. We all have a story. An all too human story. At times we run away from the very moments that will enrich our lives. One off moments of human interaction with unique individuals. I heard a good way to gauge if you are growing spiritually is to pick the most repulsive (in your eyes) person that you see all day and ask yourself can you love them as they are. I guess the answer to that is that if you are truly growing you will not find them repulsive. I have moved forward but I have much work to do still. Strangely I feel that it is easier to love the so called "repulsive people" than it is to love members of your own peer group. Probably because one sees the shadow of oneself projected in the peer group and we all need to love ourselves more. We all need to balance our shadows.

Inhibitions

I had the pleasure of watching a toddler dancing this morning on Facebook. Her grandmother, Kathy is a friend of mine that is always very actively, and positively engaged in life and as such is an interesting person to follow on Facebook. Which is more than can be said for many people that just use it to complain and waste time due to an obviously low boredom threshold. I wish that if they didn't have anything interesting to say that they would just refrain from saying the first thing that comes into their heads. That is okay in therapy but not great for sharing with the world. I love to see toddlers dancing at this age as they are totally uninhibited as yet by society mores. They just do whatever they feel and mimic anyone that seems to know what to do. We should be copying them. They have so much to teach us that we have forgotten through years of being told what is right and what is wrong. Small wonder we have become predictable and dull compared to the wonder world of the toddler. Where anything is possible. And the impossible happens every day. Toddler world is the place to be. Never does dancing get performed with such purity and fun. Dancing from the depths of their souls. In love with the fact that their bodies move in such amazing ways, a feeling that gives them immense pleasure. Look what I can do.

When did we forget how to marvel at the wonders of our bodies? When did we decide that being human was a punishment and having a body was a curse? And everything was impossible or somebody outside of ourselves fault. Toddlers are right, all is possible and the human body is an amazing gift from Mother Nature. It is up to us how we treat that gift and how we align our minds to work with our bodies to enrich our experiences throughout life. Human beings are born with limitless potential where did we lose that belief and why do we teach our children to be limited. I much prefer the optimistic attitude than the prevailing pessimism that pervades much of society these days. That is also why I like Kathy so much. She seems to be optimistic 24/7 and takes the knocks in an optimistic way. Life was never meant to be a happiness parade 24/7 but it is filled with precious moments and life lessons each and every day. Most of these moments and lessons are missed by overly distracted people trying to be something for others. Amassing a big pile of stuff seems to be a life purpose or at least a bigger and better pile than your peers. Getting better for many people is getting better stuff. It never occurs until later in life, if at all, that getting better may be something that happens inside of oneself. An awakening to what life may be about once you start to search for answers to knowing yourself and being yourself. Life then gets interesting. Loving others but not living one's life to please others or involved in some imaginary status competition in which you have totally lost your identity over the years.

Toddlers reach an age when they are taught that there is a "right" way to dance, a socially acceptable way to dance. In reality they learn that there is a socially acceptable way to do everything and that others evaluation of you is vitally important. That it is important to be good at everything and if you are not the best, at least try ones best. They are taught that life is a competition in every moment. They are compared to others and society norms constantly. They are taught to be normal and should you deviate from what is considered normal the opinion of others will punish you with exclusion from the herd. As one gets older exclusion from the herd can sound like quite an attractive proposition, but when you are young it is devastating. There are many instances when young girls have hurt themselves, even committed or attempted to commit suicide due to being sent to Coventry (ignored deliberately) at private schools or from being excluded from the popular groups.

I get to wondering why I don't evaluate (judge) Toddlers dancing the same way I have evaluated adults for their dancing over the years. I have been part of the problem that I am highlighting. I have the attitude that any guy dancing uninhibitedly and less than perfectly is a big idiot. A term my Father used over the years, we learn so much from our significant others. I have been more tolerant of women but still have been very judgemental over the years. It is possible, nay probable I have thought dancing is more of a female pastime than a thing real men do. My feeling was that they show themselves up and look foolish. They are happy and having fun and don't give a toss what I think, standing at the side frowning and evaluating as if I know the first thing about dancing. I am an introvert and probably wish I could be that person cutting loose on the dance floor. I have changed my views radically, realising that much if not most of my inherited behaviour was utter crap.

Humility is not thinking
less of yourself,
but thinking
of yourself less.

- C.S. Lewis

I have come to realise now that I am projecting my inhibitions onto them and a big dollop of projected pride also. I have learned that when something about others affects me that I need to examine myself to fix the issue or at least understand and work at balancing my psyche and the judgements fade and eventually vanish from my perception. It is myself that I am judging, no matter how hard that is to come to terms with, that is where the solution is to be found. Inside of oneself. How great is it to know that we don't need to go around evaluating and trying to change others in the world to make our world better. We just need to learn the lessons, wake up and change ourselves. Or wake up, learn the lessons and change ourselves to become more whole, a more complete person. One has to be awake first.

My toddler lesson is to let go of my pride and become humbler. Striking a balance between the opposites. That would lessen my being affected or shaped by what others may or may not be thinking. Often nothing at all, and becoming less inhibited. Humility is a strong position to live life from as nobody can hurt pride that doesn't exist at that level. These are areas I am working on and I know I am getting better and will continue to do so. If you are serious about getting better the best place to see yourself is in your evaluations of others. A great place to start is by seeing what affects you and then analysing what it is about them that is in you. What are you projecting to them? I have obviously been sold by society and significant others that being proud and having dignity meant stashing humility in my shadow bag. Now, I realise that to become a more complete person I need to introduce humility back into my psyche and attempt to strike a perfect or good enough balance to harmonise my personality. There is also the belief that dancing is for girls. I find that funny as I would consider myself quite a feminist. I must have a deep seated belief that girls dance and boys drink and tell tales. How embarrassing for me. This means that when I am in my shadow bag searching for humility I will need to dig out a little feminine shadow to balance my feminine, masculine opposites. We are all a delicate balance of everything. We are all things at once.

Exercise humility. Keep in mind that there's always someone superior than you. Even a child can teach you something new.

©QuotesEmpire.com

This highlights how every moment is a learning moment for personal spiritual growth, completing our psyches and revealing our sacred selves. All this from watching a beautiful young uninhibited toddler dancing.

 Television – Public Enemy No1

And now to re-visit the television, the goggle box. Why did I feel that is was a negative influence in my life? I would first like to mention that a typical reaction to any discussion on the evils of television is for the social unit (you & I) to justify and make light of there ever possibly being any problem with this particularly well loved and convenient time gobbling piece of technology. Therein sits the danger lost deep in the complacency of the social units. An average social unit (Jung's phrase for our roles in society when we have lost our individuality) in Britain watches the goggle box for three and a half hours per day – roughly twenty-five hours per week. Harmless enough? Right. At worse it could be considered a ridiculous waste of a life. Let's take a closer look.

> *"The individual disappears......The individual is increasingly deprived of the moral decision as to how he should live his own life, and instead is ruled, fed, clothed and educated as a social unit, accommodated in the appropriate housing unit, and amused in accordance with the standards that give pleasure and satisfaction to the masses.........As a social unit he has lost his individuality and become a mere abstract number in the bureau of statistics. He can only play the role of an interchangeable unit of infinitesimal importance"*

- Jung

Television was banned in Bhutan until, in 1999 the king decided to let television into his country. Up to that time TV had been banned as had all public advertising. Licenses were given to more than thirty cable operators. The Bhutanese could see the usual mixture of football, violence, advertising and wrestling available in most places across the world. They soaked it up like a sponge. However, the impact on their society provides an enlightening and frightening natural experiment in how technology can affect attitudes and behaviour. In the idyllic Buddhist kingdom nestling in the Himalayas soon a sharp increase in family break up, crime and drug taking was noticed. Violence in schools increased. One study by local academics showed that a third of parents preferred watching television to talking to their children. Similarly, in 1973 there were communities in Canada just being introduced to television? Research groups monitored one particular town. Social life was reduced, particularly for the old and people stopped playing sport. As television is so passive, it reduced the measured creativity of people, both young and old.

IF THE TELEVISION CRAZE CONTINUES WITH THE PRESENT LEVEL OF PROGRAMS, WE ARE DESTINED TO HAVE A NATION OF MORONS.

Television reduces social life. But it could be argued widens our experience. If television simply reflected life as it is, it would doubtless have little effect. It does not mirror life – that would be monotonous to watch. Television focuses on the extraordinary, more violence, sex, wealth, beauty and chaotic relationships than everyday life does. The wealth and beauty create discontent with what people have. A desire to steal or earn more wealth or to find a more beautiful partner. The chaos and violence makes people more willing to employ violence themselves. After a reported suicide or drama suicide more people actually take their own lives. The more television a child watches the more aggressive he becomes. The same was shown in Bhutan and Canada (Layard, 2005, p.85-90). I have previously discussed in my book Dazed and confused the hypnotic effect of television on young people (Lipton, 2009, p.132).

There has been much written on the evils of television. I have cancelled my cable and initially was astounded at how much time I have won back. Bored? The answer to that is not to watch television but rather to fill one's life with more creative pursuits. Read, meditate, and talk to one another and maybe even look at new ways to develop your life and your relationships. I once heard boredom described as a person that is not comfortable with their own company. I like that, simple thought but tough to accomplish. I hold to that idea. Learn to enjoy being with yourself and your thoughts. Learn to get comfortable with silence. One doesn't always have to fill silent moments with noise. Allow yourself the luxury of doing nothing.

I do see room for a television in my life but being able to choose selective programs commercial free is a great difficulty. Otherwise we are welcoming mind control into our homes. How can we use it and protect ourselves at the same time?

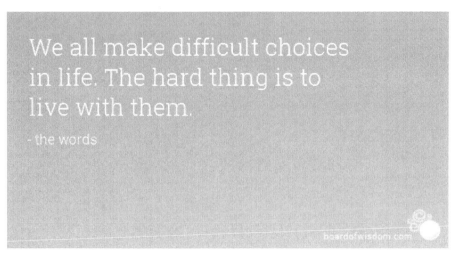

We all make difficult choices in life. The hard thing is to live with them.

- the words

boardofwisdom.com

Making The Right Choice

If you are playing Russian roulette, there is a right choice and a wrong choice. The wrong choice gets your brains blown out. Choices are rarely as simple as that, the simplest of choices with the direst of consequences. When making choices it would seem that one often assumes there is a right choice and a wrong choice. If the choice made doesn't work out as predicted, and to be fair how could it realistically? That is predicting the future and is rarely accurate. Then the chooser decides they have made the wrong choice assuming for some reason that they know how the other choice would have worked out. And it would have been better than the choice made. The possibility of either both choices being disastrous or both being perfect never seems to fit the psyche of the chooser. One is the right choice and the other is the wrong choice. One can see how this would lead a person to procrastinate. Looking for the right choice rather than just choosing the most likely suitable option and then getting on with the consequences. As for regretting the choice made, that is never a wise move. The other choice may have been better or worse, but more importantly one can never know and as such regretting the unknown is simply ridiculous. When the choice is made the other choice ceases to exist and should be regarded in this manner. There will be plenty more choices for you to think about in the future without dwelling on choices that never existed once you had made your original choice. Choose wisely and then move on to future choices. Your choice now is do I know what he is talking about or do I need to read this again? Will I regret it if I read it again? No, you made the choice, live with it.

 Contagious Happiness

Whilst talking to a friend recently the conversation turned to the subject of mood transference. My opinion, with which he disagreed, was that not only is a smile contagious to others with whom you interact, but also, by smiling when you are grumpy you will change your own mood. Our opinions differed and that is perfectly fine. My final points were that when you witness another person having totally lost control of themselves with laughter, the result is you laughing at them laughing, not being fully aware of why they laugh. The same can be said about a toddler giggling. Both truly fantastic human moments. We still did not agree. How great is it to totally lose control of your body in laughter? I, for one, do not giggle anywhere near enough. When did life become so serious? Can we ever get back to that care free giggle a day existence? I need to find my way back. My inner child is lost; it has been a long time since I was cerebrally tickled by something so much that the mere thought produced convulsions of laughter. So when did life become so serious?

> Fun is essential to mastering the serious side of life. It provides the balance that keeps us sane.
>
> *Peter Nicholls*

 When Did Life Get So Serious?

In answer to my own question, when did life become so serious? Maybe I have one possible theory, amongst many. From our earliest years as children we are told to strive for the esteem of others, to accumulate as much stuff as possible and to win friends. We are burdened with duties to perform in order to become a normal upstanding member of society. There are lessons to learn, exercises to do to be better than the rest. Children are convinced by significant others that any slip ups and happiness will be ruined. Children wake up increasingly stressed each day as their duties and the consequences of failure dawn on them. Under these circumstances spontaneous fits of the giggles become rare. In actual fact, spontaneity of any kind is rare. A predictable, machine like existence being preferred. There must be a better way. We need to ease the burden and allow children and young people to work out for themselves who they are and what they want to become. There is too much pressure from outside to become someone for others. The existentialist term for this unfortunate state is "being for others". Something we all succumb to in varying degrees. In my opinion this is when life becomes too serious.

 Freddy's Bench Press 1

Whilst at the gym yesterday, I met with Freddy. Freddy seems to have adopted me as his mentor for the moment; he picks my brain and asks my advice on all things that may make him stronger and improve his physique. Like many gym members, Freddy lets his gym identity rest largely on his ability to bench press, a favourite exercise of many men. Unusually, Julie and I do not include bench press in our workouts, as I have found from past experience that it is likely to injure my shoulders. However, it is worshipped by many gym users. As an indicator of how popular the bench press has become as an exercise, nine times out of ten in day-to-day life, upon seeing a muscular physique, the first question someone will ask is, "How much can you bench press?" That is no exaggeration. Most men have a real personal best lift and a mythological personal best lift. The mythological lift increases as they get older; hence the saying, "The older I get, the better I was." I have listened to men in the street brag to me about a bench press personal best that would be a world record if it were true. Fact: (almost) all men lie about how much they can bench press or have bench pressed. I have seen men almost come to blows in such moments. Exaggeration is commonly accepted (ignored).

Our gym managers, in their infinite wisdom, are holding a bench-
pressing competition for members. Maybe this will settle some
arguments, but I doubt it very much. It may start some more, and
we will certainly get many excuses and much blame for less than-
mythological performances. This should be a fun day with a capital
F! Incidentally, all of the guys are as nice as pie, and the bragging is
just a guy thing that even I don't fully understand – and I have
been in the gym business for over thirty-eight years. Freddy has
turned to me for help with his preparation, and even though you
could get all I know about bench pressing on the back of a postage
stamp, miraculously, he has been getting stronger as the day
approaches. He is taking this event very seriously. I see him most
days, and most days he has a question or an update on his
progress. We have discussed every eventuality – or at least I
thought we had. With less than a week to go, Freddy told me today
about what he planned to do for that week and how he was having
two days off training before the big day. In the process of working
out, I gave the thumbs-up to what he was telling me. I continued
training. I was alone today, as Julie had been called into work.

Freddy was about ten feet (three metres) away from me, also training alone, although the interaction in the gym is always very high energy amongst the regulars, and one is never really alone. Freddy moved towards me with a concerned look on his face, and he whispered very loudly, "What about the sex?" All heads turned.

"No, thanks," I said. He hesitated. I smiled, because I knew that he was asking whether abstaining would help his performance. Most of the gym heard. Remembering that this was a small local contest in a local gym for its members, Freddy was certainly thinking of everything. I replied that it was his call but that I didn't deem abstinence as essential. I told him that it might possibly make him more aggressive but that I didn't feel a lack of aggression would be a problem, with it being a contest and people watching. I pointed out that he might even become over-aroused, a psychological term for being too wound up for the sport you are participating in. Controlled aggression is what Freddy will need. I am pretty sure using the word aroused in sporting terms lost Freddy and that he was probably picturing himself bench pressing with an erection. He had a grin from ear to ear and was giggling like a schoolgirl. What did strike me after this exchange was Freddy's attention to detail for such an event and how important this part of his life was to who he was and how he wanted others to see him. It would be so easy to trivialise the whole event, and I would have been guilty, as a relatively non-macho non-bench presser, of exactly that accusation: of trivialising the whole affair and of failing to see the importance of such an event in another person's life. I understand now. I will support Freddy, win or lose, and the others in the contest and let you all know further how the day goes off. The smallest moments have the greatest impact on human lives. Seeing friendly faces in support becomes part of those small but significant moments.

Sunday morning at ten o'clock, participants and curious observers are gathering in the gym for the club bench-press competition. There are many no-shows, and nobody has seen Freddy since Wednesday. Freddy is a permanent fixture at the gym under normal circumstances. Just after 10 a.m., the door opens, and in walks Freddy with his two boys. Let the games begin. I note that all the competitors have a healthy respect for one another. There are all shapes and sizes, and body weight will be considered for all lifts. The bench to be used is surrounded by onlookers, and this is the first time most of these lifters will have experienced such an atmosphere. Nerves are likely to play a part. All look a little displaced and deal with the pressure in slightly different ways. Those with previous experience are more laid-back and relaxed. Freddy looks exposed and vulnerable, outside of his normal comfort zone, as do many others.

There are two disciplines. The first is a strict one-repetition lift with as much weight as possible, which goes against body weight. The second lift is as many repetitions as possible, with body weight. The event goes very well. Freddy places in one of the events, and all are encouraged and visibly lifted by their first competitive experience and the support they receive. They feel special. All pride remains intact, and the bench-press brotherhood is strengthened by the experience. It is notable that for most of the week leading up to the event participants were visibly boosted by the experience.

Sadly, and true to form, the no-shows tried to steal the thunder, yapping about how they would have won but had been unable to make the contest. The phrase "put up or shut up" springs to mind. It was a good event and, all in all, a particularly human morning. The event was not at all the carnage one might have anticipated considering the gym hostilities previously experienced. Just in closing, it is worth mentioning that, compared to what one particular lifter boasts he can lift loudly and regularly in his day-to-day workouts (his mythological best), his actual lift was some 40 kg less. But at least he attended and placed well. Interestingly, all boasted best lifts were down accordingly once actions were needed to replace words. We do love to spin yarns.

 Soul Shrug and Smile

Dealing with many, often very negative people in any given day can be challenging to say the least. We find that developing our own little ways such as the soul shrug to ease our way through the angst moments makes the whole journey through life more interesting and can turn iffy moments into precious moments by changing ourselves and our thought process in the moment. All with an inner shrug and smile. Body language is all there is.

The method that we use to free ourselves from ego and to get better in the moment has to be quick it is our soul shrug. Ordinarily a shrug shows a disinterested attitude. The soul shrug is exactly the opposite. It is a loving acceptance of what is and a letting go of any negative, ego driven and automatic reaction in a split second. For example – upon getting caught in the rain a smile and a soul shrug works miracles. Another example – another person or their ego is gossiping, complaining and generally being negative and turbulent, attempting to draw you in to their low frequency energy. A smile and a soul shrug will release you from your egos desire to join in the negativity. Try it, next time you meet a stranger and they complain about the weather, resist the temptation to be negative about a situation you can never change and just smile and shrug. A point here is that a soul shrug is not visible to others, it is an attitude of acceptance and release. I actually physically shrug with my eyebrows whilst smiling. The soul shrug has real power once you master it's quick and effective use. We see it as a positive coat of armour for when we are being bombarded by negativity either from within ourselves via our own ego or from without via another's ego.

This is simple but very effective. The other person often smiles right there with you. Try it when you feel the pressure welling up inside of you. Let it go.

Searching for Happiness

Mechanically our compulsions make us feel that our happiness is to be sought outside of ourselves. Our aspirations and passions push us to look outwards aided by a consumer culture that reinforces these erroneous beliefs, even when there is nothing to excite us. A myriad of external objects tempt and seduce us, even when we are not thinking about them they are thrust into our immediate consciousness via the media constantly. We are surrounded by these objects from dawn till dusk and then probably dream about having them. Wise men, self-help books and even our own reason may tell us to look inside of ourselves to search for happiness within our own souls. Scared of what we might find. We never look. We simply don't believe them. We are too busy and distracted by our search amongst the endless array of external objects and situations.

111

When you think about the moments that still make you smile, they are never expensive and always priceless. A toddler's giggle. A baby's smile. A random act of kindness from a stranger or to a stranger. Precious moments are everywhere. You just have to wake up and notice them.

> Most people are searching for happiness outside of themselves. That's a fundamental mistake. Happiness is something you are, and it comes from the way you think.

 Just Perfect

Perfection or the ideal, whose idea exactly is the perfection human beings strive so hard to attain. Well without apportioning any blame the ideologies and images which portray perfection to us need to be unattainable, that way we all continue to spend our money on achieving the impossible. The media and associated industries need us to be dissatisfied. Let us take a look at perfection in a different way. If man had a hand in designing nature which he often does with his landscaped gardens, all would be symmetry, straight lines, ordered colours and uniformity in appeal. Try to imagine a single tree designed by man and then a forest of those trees with accompanying flora and man designed wild life.

Have you got that image? Now think of the rain forest with all of the seemingly random shapes, colours, sizes, the amazing waterfalls and diverse wildlife. Which is more perfect to you? Without doubt, Mother Nature can never be surpassed even when man has the plans and blueprint she still remains unsurpassed. So, this would indicate that man's idea of perfection is never as perfect as a Mother Nature original. Then maybe we would come to the conclusion that man's idea of perfection is always a pale imitation of the original. Now for a moment, holding the image of a man made forest with identical symmetrical trees in nice neat rows, picture a main street in any town or city. Now imagine, the ideal body image for men and women portrayed in the media for this era, visualise everyone has finally achieved this look. Each and every man, woman and child identical. Is that perfection? Now imagine the same scene our creator's way, all of us different, unique and happy that way. We can all be fit and strong but just the way we are

"I always find beauty
in things that are
odd & imperfect-
they are much more
interesting."

MARC JACOBS

shaped is our original and individual perfection. We are created whole and perfect, then we tend to abuse that creation with poor nutrition habits and no exercise. We each have a genetic potential that is perfect and fits our world as does every piece of the rainforest jigsaw. The vision of perfection sold to us by the media is simply false and unrealistic. Perfection is surely reaching Mother Nature's genetic potential for our unique self, through exercise, nutrition, peace of mind and good habits. We are already perfect creations but often we mess up that gift with poor and misguided lifestyle habits. Love who you are and be the best version possible of you, not a media creation. Next time you are wishing for that media created perfection, think, of the rainforest or any of Mother Nature's creations of which you are one and find your inspiration. Then find joy in the knowledge that the creator got it right and you can never be improved upon. Work every muscle in your body as Nature intended, they are part of your body for a reason, to be used. Don't store fuel (fat) you are unlikely to have any future need for that stored fuel. Get moving, get happy and laugh at society's idea of what is ideal. Embrace your Natural shape, exude confidence, love your wrinkles and hair, and see aging as the amazing time of life that it really is. Above all appreciate the whole of the human race as potentially perfect just the way they were created. Never lose sight of your perfection.

> *"We but half express ourselves, and are ashamed of that divine idea which each of us represents.........What I must do is all that concerns me, not what the people think.....It is easy in the world to live after the world's opinion.... It is easy in solitude to live after our own...Nothing can bring you peace*

but yourself. Nothing can bring you peace but the triumph of principles" - Emerson

If we can apply this to our thoughts and actions, then maybe we will become the unique individuals we are intended to be and recognize the same in others and applaud individuality and the right to be different in all people.

THE BIGGEST CHALLENGE OF LIFE IS TO BE YOURSELF IN A WORLD THAT IS TRYING TO MAKE YOU LIKE EVERYONE ELSE.

 Go On, Smack Your Lips One More Time.

For some reason we seem disproportionately aggravated by people that chomp food vociferously and slurp drinks noisily. Often to the point of wishing to choke them until they quieten. I have a friend that exclaimed how his parents annoyed him by the way they slurped their tea. He said this is why he never drank tea. Julie and I looked at one another as this particular friend exhibits the most noise ever recorded by a human being and most of the animal kingdom, when he eats or drinks. We remained silent. The time was not right. My opportunity arose at a later date whilst discussing how what we hate most in others are the things we are guiltiest of ourselves. I used his parents eating noises as an example. He was shocked and surprised but did laugh. He looked over to Julie to confirm his worst fears. He wondered how he must have been annoying others for years without realising. He would now be more conscious although it has not made an ounce of difference. He is still very loud. Should we accept that we are disproportionately aggravated by such small matters, accept it as natural and give in to such strange behaviour? My thought is no, we should recognise how trivial and insignificant the behaviour is and rise above being annoyed by such inconsequential matters. I use the moments to reassert a little control over my emotions. I have a similar issue with my dog Jake, barking. If I am getting to wound up over it then it is time for a reality check, a shrug and to regain some self-control. Such matters cannot be permitted to influence our lives or control our moods. That is just too weak and frankly a little ridiculous.

The Courage to Create

On the themes of difference, individuality and creativity I sat pondering over yet another advertisement for a creative writing course. Is such a course a paradox? I know that in an out of control capitalist society selling dreams such as becoming a bestselling author can be big business but surely the very notion of creativity is, that it cannot, or should not, be a systemised learned behaviour. Good writing comes from the heart riding on individual wisdom through knowledge. Knowledge becomes wisdom once reason is applied and through experience. I simply do not understand the human obsession with creating uniformity and sameness. Or to that matter the over emphasis on the technical side of writing that eclipses any unique differences. How does this sound? If writing communicates, teaches, entertains or inspires and on rare occasions all four then surely that is success. That sounds right to me, how about you? All humans have their own built in limitations, known as one's facticity in existentialist terms and lots of them, race, class, when and where born, conditioning, life memories and perceptions, the list just goes on, so why place even more limitations on the creative process. We are all very different so why not stay that way. 'How to' books for creative processes? I am not convinced. My personal philosophy has become to avoid structured guidance as much as possible for the reason that it stifles creativity and produces writers the same as other writers.

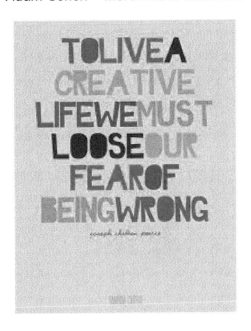

Could it be argued that for any venture to be creative it's all about the journey on a self-made trail? Creativity is not about using the same trail as others. Create, don't mimic or conform. A little hope that you will find a publisher appreciative enough and brave enough to back your uniqueness will help also. Sadly, the bottom line rules most decisions. Conformity will invariably produce mediocrity, whereas creativity will turn up a full range of standards from very poor to very good and even genius often by the same person. Creativity encourages experimentation. Both successful and unsuccessful. With the fear removed creative individuals can let themselves go. Maybe the only rule should be "There are no rules".

 Label Your Idea for Effect - Flexitarianism

Give a behaviour a trendy new name and a whole new market will be created. Currently we have vegetarians and the rest. Many people do not eat meat every day but would not be found shopping for vegetarian options as many people think that is a bit quirky and vegetarians are a little strange, pale and undernourished. Heaven forbid they are seen with those food choices in their shopping baskets. This is the cue for the clever marketing man at a top UK meat-free food company to commission a study obviously to say just what the company wants it to say. That the number of people turning to meat-free options will double in the next year and that flexitarianism will soon be a mega-trend. That will obviously clear the way for all the cool people that eat meat just now and again to shop for options in the flexitarian (meat-free) section of their local supermarket. For many the no go area of years gone by. When someone labels a behaviour as cool and it is already your own behaviour, others will surely join you in that behaviour. Very few people eat meat every single day. There are already millions of people exhibiting the infrequent meat eating behaviour being named flexitarianism. I would include myself in that group. New label affixed the gates are now open for one to consider buying meat-free options or at least that is the plan and hope of our well known meat-free company. I suppose the vegetarian options section in the supermarkets will be renamed "vegetarian & flexitarian options". A place for all the cool flexitarians to meet and mingle. A readymade customer base being redirected to meat-free options. Brilliant. And in this case quite a positive healthy cause, although some meat free options are loaded with calories. It would be great if marketing men always had such worthy ends to their cunning ploys. They do not.

The Human Collective – Science Fact

In my younger days I went through a stage of watching Star Trek. Looking back, I remember a race called the Borg. The Borg travelled through space assimilating any life form that they encountered. Any and all life forms that were different were taken on board their ship and turned into Borg. A cyborgs race. Assimilated into the Borg collective. Years later, I am a bit slow at times, it occurs to me that this is in a subtler way exactly what is happening to the human race. At least the Borg were obvious and one could resist. Assimilation into the human collective is much more deceitful or subtle and thus meets less resistance.

You are probably thinking I have finally gone totally insane, maybe, but let me explain further.

There are limitations placed upon the power of state and governments when it comes to forceful interference into individual lives. This means that to control the masses the authorities must act upon the choices, wishes, values and conduct of the individual in an indirect, some would say devious manner. That's control over you and me. No exceptions. Knowledge and expertise provides the essential distance between the formal laws, courts and police and the shaping of the activities of citizens. If an expert says it is so, then it must be correct. The control is achieved not by the threat of violence or constraint, but by the way of persuasion built in to contrived truths, the anxieties stimulated by its norms, and the attraction exercised by the images of the life and the self it offers to us even though more often they are a lie and illusory. The government works by acting at a distance upon people's choices, creating a balance between the attempts of individuals to make life rewarding for themselves, and the state values of consumption, profitability, efficiency and social order. The irony is that we believe, in making our individuality the principle of our personal lives, our behavioural systems, and our political evaluations, that we are freely choosing our freedom. Whilst in reality we are" freely" choosing exactly what we are being brainwashed to choose or to put it milder conditioned to choose and at the same time policing others to remain within the norms also by way of our obvious indignation, when one should do otherwise (public opinion). The perfect crime.

You may still be thinking I am crazy.

Is your television bigger than your bookcase and if you have a bookcase is it full of junk literature such as celebrity biographies, cookery books, Jackie Collins or equivalent and maybe even that 50 shades junk? That doesn't qualify either as literature or as a bookcase sorry. Do you watch Big Brother, Dancing on Ice, X Factor, Strictly Ballroom, and any other pop shows that are top of the viewing charts? Do you take holidays once or twice a year, mostly abroad? Do you have you an iPhone or similar? Do you have brands that you prefer in most shopping? Must you have the latest and newest gadget whatever? Do you celebrate, Halloween, fireworks night, and any other commercially recognised celebration? Did you wave a British flag for the Olympics and for the jubilee with everyone else? Do you hold any opinions that are actually your own or are your opinions by an amazing coincidence the same as many others? Do you do the lottery every week, in the hope that more money will be where you will find happiness? Do you wish for another life or to be rich?

You have already been assimilated. But you are not alone.

The bad news is that most of are already assimilated and socialised as the governments technologies of domination and social control work their devious magic. Condemned to live little more than robot lives. The good news is that once we find out we can choose otherwise. But more bad news I am afraid. Living as an individual outside of the norms is a tough place to live. As an example. A young friend recently received a phone call from his friends telling him that they had booked their next holiday, including him. However, he did not want to go for his own reasons. Even though they used a voucher belonging to him they believed he was wrong not to want to go. He was summonsed to a meeting and tempers flared. They simply could not accept that he did not want to be part of that particular herd for that particular holiday. Laughable? Yes, if it wasn't so sad. One doesn't have to look far for this type of pressure in anyone's life. Take a look at your own life. How much control do other people have over your choices? The way you dress, behave, socialise, exercise and the list just goes on and on. Once you become aware you can begin to master the art of individuality once more and find a more authentic self waiting. However, the easy option is the comfort in conformity of the human collective, the herd. But that is not living.

That is hardly a life at all. We live once, make it the life you want to live not the fake promise of a happier more fulfilling life by capitalist consumer media to be found when you buy more stuff, which just never materialises and as I will show later, has the opposite effect. We exist to serve the economy, rather than the other way around. The same life as every other robot. Start to search for your own path. But beware as the price of living your own life among a human collective, of behaving differently is a constant battle for your individuality. A constant confusion as to why you are not as predictable, a fear of you as different, as unique and finally as an authentic individual changing and becoming anew each day. This is the path I have chosen and have no regrets. A path that has many rewards and just feels intuitively right. I will continue to tell you the battles I am fighting day to day. Currently I have got rid of the television (for now). As you read on you will find how I have coped and how much hold your television may be having over your life but also how much it may be stopping you from living a much better life as a human being.

To summarise this section with regards to social theory and attempt to make it a bit more understandable. Social theories adopt alternative positions to charting the intricacies of personal experience. The conviction of selfhood is examined evenly between those that deny the agency (choice) of human subjects and argue in favour of the individuals being determined by social structures as discussed above, in one camp. And those that celebrate the authenticity and creativity of the self in the other. From my perspective, I believe the social structure side is winning and taking our freedom in most cases. No surprise as most are not even aware of the situation. Does our education system deliberately avoid such conjecture I wonder? I believe also that we, as unique individuals, can fight back and carve out a good life with meaning once our eyes and minds have been opened. The choice is to live your life comfortably as a puppet, some might harshly say Muppet, bent on accumulating more stuff and in search of the illusory Promised Land. That is the plight of the majority of mankind. The alternative choice is to live your life authentically and free with your eyes and mind wide open and preferably stuck in a book enlightening yourself even further or out communing with nature and other human beings that are out amongst the robots, puppets and Muppets somewhere. The latter being a constant focus on not being sucked back into the human (Borg) collective. The magnetic pull to assimilation never ceases. Never.

 Age

I find myself reflecting on age today and intrigued by the general preoccupation with age in society as a way of labelling and categorising differences and attaching standard limitations for either young or older citizens that they invariably assume and make a reality. Once you begin to think on this, examples begin to spring up everywhere. From sport on television to general everyday interaction with others. Maybe you have already come across some sort of age bias during your life, if you have yet to experience it, rest assured we will all be subject to some sort of age label that will work to limit us in some way or another. We will all be considered either too old or too young at some time in our lives. I would rank this preoccupation with age somewhere up there with the British preoccupation with the weather. It does not seem possible that one person can interact with another without needing to know their age. On the television age is always part of any sports person's introductory profile. At once this leads to the inevitable stereotyping abstractions that follow the labelling process. And the individual begins to become invisible. What one actually becomes is a gendered object of a certain age assuming all of that objects fixed characteristics. How often are we deprived of seeing the talented youngster in sport because of the obsession with age as a contributing factor to their performance? How many athletes and generally people in many walks of life are socially conditioned to know for sure when they are too old. Not through any real reason other than a conditioned belief which is reinforced with alarming frequency in day to day life. A belief incorporated into the collective psyche of an entire population. A limiting belief that does not serve us well. A belief that takes away our freedom.

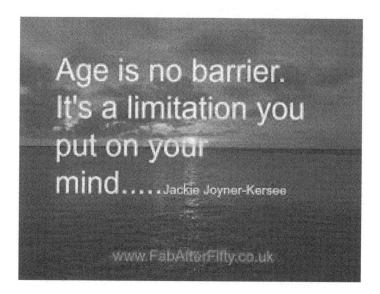

Chatterbox Self

We all know what is like to be in a conversation and feel that what one has to say is so important that listening to the other person's chatter seems to be getting in the way. I remember reading that if you could see people's energy when they were in a conversation that most of the time it would be a battle to be the person with the most energy left at the finish of the communication. As the battle for supremacy leans one way then the other. Sapping the others energy and boosting one's own. We can all commit the error of believing we are the only ones with anything worthy to say. Never listening and only using the gaps in our speech to think of what to say next. Very often talking over the other person and interrupting them (pride). The enthusiasm and excitement of the exchange being too much for the restraint needed for a compassionate communication. We have heard enough about them now let's talk about ourselves. To talk about oneself a lot can also be a means of concealing oneself.

"My short-term goal is to bluff my way through this job interview. My long-term goal is to invent a time machine so I can come back and change everything I've said so far."

Could it be argued that if you want to create a good impression then a strategy of not speaking would best serve ones needs. We have heard the line that we have been given two ears and only one mouth so we can listen twice as much as we talk. The point being we need to listen more and that listening is where the art of conversation and communication begins. Only a small percentage of what we say contributes to our communication, there is another 93% that goes on away from the chatter. That is wasted if we never know when to shut up or when to be in the present moment and become aware of all the subtle nuances that occur between two compassionate human beings. Any person serious about getting better needs to address their communication skills as a matter of priority. I have much to learn in this respect but I find that if I just think to myself that what I have to say is not really as important as making each other feel appreciated and valued. The connection is where the value is to be found in our meetings with others.

Spending more time silently communicating and listening to others is the place to start. This subject has been covered masterfully by Andrew Newberg, M.D., and Mark Robert Waldman in the book Words Can Change Your Brain. I would recommend this book to anyone looking to explore the rich subject of human communication in order to get better. I can think of others that leave me shell shocked when our turbulent interaction is complete. I breathe a sigh of relief and think how the communication was just plain hard work. I would describe these meetings as conversations between two egos. When one person awakes the ego in the other and the battle begins. Ironically for me and maybe you also this is the case with members of my own family. Ram Dass is quoted as saying that "if you think you are enlightened go and spend the weekend with your family." I understand that challenge completely and also understand that the challenge is inside of each of us as individuals capable of change and not in changing others to meet our communication demands.

129

It would be much easier to become enlightened in a controlled environment in your home or on the top of a mountain somewhere. But where is the challenge in that. It is not really possible to be one with all of mankind if you avoid them like the plague. That applies to all of life, so if you are selective in your likes and dislikes of animals, insects etc. that is not really in the spirit of spiritual growth either. I would say that whether you talk to all of life is entirely up to you but there is much study into the fact that plants are aware of your intentions and as such there is more consciousness around than one may have been led to believe to this point.

All of my plants have names and I can be caught regularly chatting away to all kinds of life. What is there to lose? They may not speak English but if there is genuine emotional intention behind your words they may be understanding you much better than you think. To be totally honest it is much easier to love plants and animals than it is some humans. It is a good place to practice and they rarely answer back or manipulate you to bait your ego. There have been times when Smudge and Jake my terriers have gotten me to react less than perfectly (anger). The way I see it if I can't react compassionately with two adorable small black dogs with the sole intention of getting food, fuss and walks, I have little chance of remaining Zen out amongst the ego dominated world that we all have to operate in. The art is to remain calm and in control at all times no matter what the provocation may be. Excuse me, I left the subject towards the end. However, it is all relevant to our progress.

The Super-Social Self

Something like 93% of communication happens without words, with body language and by processes that we as yet do not fully understand. We are remarkable and complicated organisms and we know very little about ourselves. Are we heading in the wrong direction with communications away from developing our unique abilities in favour of handing over the task to impersonal machines and endangering losing our true human abilities, as surplus to requirement forever?

We all know somebody or we are that somebody that has literally hundreds of "friends" on various social media sites but never leaves the comfort of their front room without taking their contacts with them. Now! I understand that we are living in the golden age of communication but I for one believe that human beings are actually losing the ability to communicate face to face with others. When all of our so called friends are on our computer or we carry them with us on our phone when we go out into potential meeting new people situations, how can that ever be deemed social? I get fed up of saying good morning to people that have headphones or their phone stuck on their person and are oblivious and totally unaware of the world around them. Are we in danger of becoming more machine than human? No longer in control of the situation. Can we live without our phone? If the answer is an unhesitating no, then we have a problem. I could understand a reaction of "well it might be difficult at times because certain important people expect me to be available but I could re-condition them to contact me at set times so I don't walk around constantly attached to my phone. So! Yes, I could take my life back." I am afraid that the first answer is the dominant answer. We! My friends are owned by the phone companies. We have given much of our freedom away. Not to worry though because we will realize many other ways we have lost our freedom in the coming pages and we are not alone. I wonder how many dreadfully lonely people there are with long lists of friends on a computer yet not a real friend in the world. I decided here that social networking sites are places where you can quite readily witness all of the seven deadly sins within a very short space of time. Try for yourself. Greed, anger, pride, sloth, lust, gluttony and envy. There are some slightly different variations but these are commonly known. Sadly, most of these are witnessed on social networking sites and actually seem to be revered behaviours in capitalist society. The seven deadly sins have become normal in today's society.

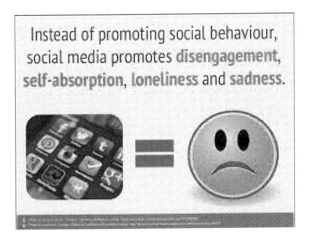

Is there a way to live in this world but not become a product of it?

Maybe having lived the answer to that question we will have lived a good life.

Smarty-Pants Self

With the availability of the worldwide web information has become a valuable resource and even the least bookish of people can seem to be well read. The problem with this is that the information has no value and is offered in isolated sound bites to make the know it all seem smart. The thoughts expressed are owned as personal opinions. They are then passed on out of context and with very little thought past the belief that it must be a fact and that elevates the smarty pants above you. Smarty pants rely on your being suitably impressed and not expanding the topic that they are masquerading as authorities on. The simplest form of the smarty pants is the weather forecaster. Rather than just accept the weather as it comes, accepting what is, we seem to need to know in advance and analyse each and every day according to whether we approve or disapprove of what we hear. In the UK we all seem to be very proud of our forecasting ability and are often very controlled by our weather conditions. This preoccupation with the weather succeeds in taking us away from the present moment and encourages wanting something less than what is. Add to this the almost universal belief that there is good and bad weather and you can see why the discontent caused by many of the forecasts could be a real cause for concern. Tell yourself the story about how fantastic all of our weather conditions are and the world takes on a whole different perspective.

Another favourite is the person that has acquired or swallowed a book of quotes and fires their wisdom at you constantly either in person or through the social media. The odd positive quote or advice about the weather can be very helpful to illustrate a point but not when taken as anything more than the product of shared knowledge through reading and only when appropriate. The fact that the original quote was not theirs never seems to feature in their thoughts. Possibly because they do not feel the need to have any original thoughts. Why think when others have done all the thinking for you. More often than not smarty pants are unaware of the background of their wisdom or the richness contained in the words they speak when used in the correct context. I am guilty of this at times and I have friends that base their whole personality on coming up with the right quote daily or proud that they got the weather forecast correct (I told you so – smugly) even though they repeated it straight off the television or radio report. That always makes me smile. We are all funny creatures at times. The worrying aspect of all of this is that we can all be sucked into this behaviour so easily. Becoming as sheep all following the lead of the others.

The smarty pants really comes into their own when they are able to gazump everything that you say or have done or that you know. Gazumping is a word that came to light in the real estate industry. It is when a buyer offers more than the asking price to break into a deal that has already been struck. I believe in some areas there now has to be a signed agreement early in proceedings to limit gazumping. We all know somebody that gazumps everything that is said or done. Anything you can do I have done or can do better. Or that's enough talk about you let's talk about me.

One of the smarty pants favourite haunts is pub quizzes or game shows on the television where they can use their extensive library of useless facts to amaze and astound those so easily impressed. I can think of one such television program appropriately called egg heads in which the 'stars' of the show not only give the answer but then take every opportunity to show off with extra useless facts. Having to be silenced as they sit with a smug look on their faces. A greater show of hubris (pride) I have never witnessed. The title of the show would indicate a slightly ridiculous side to this show that the contestants are far too thick skinned to feel the least bit embarrassed by. The responsibility of those with genuine intelligence is to use it to guide and help society and themselves, not to show off shamelessly for a teatime television audience with far too much time on their hands. I remember hearing once the sentence that if a person thinks they are enlightened then they most certainly are not. I would think that one could substitute the word intelligent for the word enlightened and be accurate. Intellectual potential is a personal potential for us all and whilst it can be used to motivate and encourage just the same as our physical potential, it should never be used to elevate oneself above any other person. Humility is the target here. We are all equally human.

Whether you are smart, fit or have a great body according to the ideals always use the gifts to help others realize their own perfection. I have a saying – And yes it is original or as original as words can ever be. **Getting better for me is holding the intention to be the perfect fit in the perfect universe and to help others realize they also are the perfect fit in the perfect universe wherever we are now.** You will read this often in my writing. I am considering it for the title of the book. It would have to be a big book. You could call it my mission statement. It covers my behaviour standards and growth for myself and my aims of compassion for others and all of life. I feel it is a great philosophy to create a life purpose around and to help myself to keep growing by constant awareness of others. It is not as simple as it sounds as you will find out as you continue your journey through life with the aim of getting better. For me it is a zig zag journey towards getting better. As with all goals there is never a straight line to the goal. Constant reflection on the lessons life offers up is the only way forward. There are many highs and many lows to be contemplated but the path is always left open. The door to getting better never ever closes to anyone. The journey is easier if we all help one another to realise our potential.

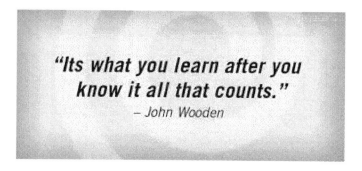

> *"Its what you learn after you know it all that counts."*
> – John Wooden

The Spiritual / Religious Self

It is easy to think that if a person comes across as spiritual or religious that they have overcome the problems the rest of us have with the ego personalities dominating our lives. Think again. Where better for the ego to hide than behind the apparent solution to its destruction. Is the person that has a massive cross hanging around their neck on the outside of their clothing and that continuously quotes the bible in conversations really free from ego? I know that person and I can tell you the ego is more dominant then I have ever seen.

Take it a step further, how many religious leaders are actually worthy of the title and how many are playing a role that they feel frees them from the egos grasp when in actual fact they are merely play acting and hunting for power and prestige. Hidden in plain sight. Does an authentic spiritual or devoutly religious being need to parade themselves as such?

137

In my home town in the UK we have a guy that dresses in Buddhist garb and parades around in public juggling two balls in his hand. He is to be seen everywhere and I am afraid all I see is an ego that wants to be the centre of attention amongst people that dress in conventional clothing and go about their business in a much less obvious way. He may be a very fine human being but I am sure he has some way to go in awareness and acceptance of his ego behaviour to reach true spiritual enlightenment. I like to think that true enlightenment and love will not be so readily advertised and used to elevate one above others. There is another gentleman that walks around with a long staff, dressed in robes more suited to a time gone by and he can be found praying in the most unlikely places. I think the word I am looking for is inconspicuous, and he is not. It is my belief that a truly spiritual person will be conspicuous by their loving presence and not by their different clothing and odd behaviour. Odd, by the behaviour norms of the society they are living in. Both of these gents may be perfectly at home and normal in a different culture, a culture that follows these behaviours but here and now, all it does is say loudly, look at me. Many people in the past and present have, and are still, hiding behind a set of hypocritical values that do not ring true when all that they really stand for and celebrate is separation. Any group that celebrates themselves as good, against others as bad, will always fail when the unity of mankind is the only way the planet and mankind will be saved.

I do understand enthusiasm about a set of thoughts that one might like at any given moment but I feel that creating a physical manifestation of those thoughts is a little extreme and the thoughts then take on the power of an identity which then becomes more important than just liking thoughts and becomes part of that person's identity. This leads to narrow mindedness and an unwillingness to open one's mind to the constant change and evolution that our thoughts must be open to for our entire lives.

Science, religion and spirituality are progressing along a path that will forever change the way we think about our roles on this planet and the biggest challenge to that evolution are the narrow minded and dogmatic ideologies that many humans are clinging to as part of who they believe they are. There needs to be a – take what is working and move onwards and upwards attitude – or we will forever be stuck fighting the wars of the past over what are insignificant details that have grown over the years because people just won't let it go and move on. Any truly religious message has been lost amongst human pride, greed and power seeking individuals. Our ego fuelled friends above may seem harmless but on a much larger global scale the results are catastrophic. Religion means to re-bond or to re-connect. I don't see that happening. I just see separation. Religion is failing in its goal. Any 'us and them' attitude will forever bring the same miserable results that human history demonstrates so readily and the daily news reinforces on an hourly basis. When any human thinks they are better than another at the core of their being the result is invariably what you see in the news and all around you every day. Here the greatest sin is pride where there needs to be humility. Yes, that is a challenge.

True religion is real living;
living with all one's soul,
with all one's goodness and
righteousness.

quotespedia.info   Albert Einstein

Religion is best when it is not being talked about or labelled but rather obvious by the actions of compassionate human beings with all of life. There used to be a line used before children gained some empowerment that went like this –" kids should be seen and not heard" – for me that is what religion should be about "religion should be seen and not heard". Stop talking about the good and just do it.

 ## What If?

I would like to relate one of my major concerns in trying to motivate others to making even the smallest changes in their lives, to improve the chances of mankind, to contribute just because contribution feels very good indeed. My issue is that it is easier for me to voice commitment to any great cause than it is to make a difference to one individual human being. My ultimate frustration would be that every single individual on the planet becomes aware of what goes on behind his or her back, and the vast majority elect to do nothing. Each decides to wait for others to make a difference first.

My ray of hope? It is to offer up, by example, so many small changes that everybody can at least make the tiniest personal statement by their actions. I want to get the ball rolling. Maybe we will make a ripple that eventually, through others conforming, will become a tidal wave of change demonstrating the peaceful power of the masses for controlling their own destiny. Ironic, indeed, if we were to rely on conformist behaviour to ultimately reach our goals!

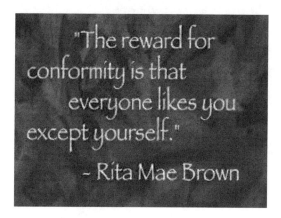

"The reward for conformity is that everyone likes you except yourself."

- Rita Mae Brown

Society needs both conformists and non-conformists, of that there can never be doubt. The danger is that we are losing our exceptional individuals to outright societal conformist behaviour. As in everything, there must be an effective balance maintained, and currently the trend is for individuals to be ineffective, as the automatons rule – or should I say "are ruled"? We must have some power against the warring self-serving governments and the greedy, profit-mongering stinkers if humanity is to have any hope of freedom in the future.

The current state of affairs is that the majority of mankind have sold their souls for stuff and gadgets while believing in their freedom, but that very freedom has been traded for a materialistic future of predictable behaviour from a robotic society. I often talk to people who are becoming increasingly aware of their conditioned existence. These people are sure that there is more to life than the non-stop consumption that fills their lives. Could it be that human beings will eventually need to be human, containing an inbuilt drive to escape control of machines and break free to a more meaningful life? Do we have a natural drive that is being suppressed in generations now but may just need to explode into new life?

The ruling classes and profit-mongers may have underestimated the situation. The future will be interesting. It is all very well putting technology in the hands of babes, to line your pockets well into the future, but what of the human instincts? Where do they go, the young humans that grow up with that nagging feeling there is more and eventually find out they have been exploited out of their humanity for another's gain? They have been forced to develop in a certain way because of the greed of an economic system that no longer works for humans or cares about their development over and above the fact that each young human must feel the need to have the latest technology for his entire life. Humans feel naked if they are not surrounded by their high-tech toys. How long will it be before those same toys do actually become physically attached?

Technology is already psychologically attached to most humans. One can witness it spreading throughout society on even the shortest walk. There are countless examples of technology ruling the vacant-looking weak human being with false promise of happiness, some bright shiny lights, and beeping noises. They are looking for happiness outside of themselves in their ever-growing pile of stuff. Pathetic! But worse than that is being hopelessly exploited by greedy pigs (sorry, real pigs) that know exactly what they are doing and at what cost to the individual.

 Dare to Create

On the themes of difference, individuality, and creativity, I sat pondering over yet another advertisement for a creative-writing course. Is such a course a paradox? I know that in an out-of-control capitalist society, selling dreams such as becoming a bestselling author can be big business, but surely the very notion of creativity is that it cannot, or should not, be a systemised learned behaviour. Good writing comes from the heart, riding on individual wisdom through knowledge. Knowledge becomes wisdom once reason is applied and through experience. I simply do not understand the human obsession with creating uniformity and sameness or, for that matter, the overemphasis on the technical side of writing that eclipses any unique differences.

How does this sound? If writing communicates, teaches, entertains, or inspires, and on rare occasions all four, then surely that is success. That sounds right to me; how about you? All humans have their own built in-limitations, known in existentialist terms as their facticity, and lots of them. They include race, class, when and where born, conditioning, life memories and perceptions – the list just goes on, so why place even more limitations on the creative process? We are all very different, so why not stay that way? "How-to" books for creative processes? I am not convinced.

Be courageous
and try to write
in a way that
scares you a little.

—*Holley Gerth*

My personal philosophy has become to avoid structured guidance as much as possible for the reason that it stifles creativity and produces writers the same as other writers. Could it be argued that for any venture to be creative it's all about the journey on a self-made trail? Creativity is not about using the same trail as others. Create, don't mimic or conform. A little hope that you will find a publisher appreciative enough and brave enough to back your uniqueness will help also. Sadly, the bottom line rules most decisions. Conformity will invariably produce mediocrity, whereas creativity will turn up a full range of standards, from very poor to very good and even genius, often by the same person. Creativity encourages experimentation, both successful and unsuccessful. With the fear removed, creative individuals can let themselves go. Maybe the only rule should be "There are no rules."

Waffling On

As you are aware, Julie and I had parked the car away for the summer on May 14 and were walking about five miles per day. In fact, we had discussed it and would have been happy to remain car-less, as the positive effects on body composition and fitness, not to mention the peace of mind from the general slowing down of life, were benefits not to be given back over to the alternative of a hostile, lazy-arsed life in the metal box. However, Julie attained a new position in a company some miles away that was not readily accessible by either bike, on foot, or even by public transport at the times when she needed to travel. The car had to be raised from slumber. I have still not driven for the first week. I am resisting, although I know and accept that I will at some time begin to use it once more.

I have known for many years now that in order to succeed in breaking any habit, I have to totally take the temptation from my life. The best example is those who attempt to diet and eat healthier when they are surrounded by junk food. We do not even attempt to start a new eating plan until the house and environments that we operate from can be perfectly controlled, or at least any stumbling points minimised.

As you can tell by now I am proud of my more active lifestyle. I will not now easily give up my new walking legs. Each morning I walk to the gym just after six o'clock with the dogs, Smudge and Jake (Jacob), happily trotting along. I meet Julie at the gym at 7 a.m., and the dogs wait in the car until we are finished. Julie then leaves for work, and I walk home with the dogs. This will change again soon, as Julie's current daytime hours are only for a short period. We will have a rethink when she eventually goes onto her night-shift pattern. Julie is excited about her new possibilities with work and her independence but a little disappointed that she misses out on the walking. It makes me smile, that healthy change of attitude, with a twenty-first century person envying another not because of his stuff but because of the joy of walking.

Most others think one must be poor or drunk or that there must be a fuel shortage if you mention walking. When did walking become a dirty word rather than reason to elevate your status? Jimmy, our training partner, has the choice to ride with Julie or to walk with me, and he chooses to walk, purely for the human experience it has become for him and a change in his way of thinking. I have been training the dogs to walk off the lead. Today I actually forgot the leads and didn't realise my error until I started my return journey. They are learning well; it is a busy route with many roads to cross. I am even being asked how I trained them. They are gaining admirers on our walks – yet another benefit of walking as opposed to driving to the park.

As I make the return journey home, I am walking past queues of traffic, with many drivers busy texting. I thank my lucky stars that I no longer find myself watching time and life hurtling past whilst sitting angry, bored, or just plain nonplussed in traffic. I would hate to know just how much time I have wasted in traffic over the years. I would urge all humans who spend precious hours in traffic, or in travel queues generally going nowhere fast, to search hard for a solution to that tragic waste of life time. Find a solution, and don't give up until you win back those hours. Quite often people travel great distances for more money or more material gain. Looked at differently, that is actually selling your life. I wonder how many of the same individuals would choose to purchase rather than sell their precious time later in life? It seems that life and time only become valuable when we have less of both. Prior to that awakening, it would appear that material gain or what I like to call "acquiring more stuff" is more important than life itself. Really?

Julie is loving her new job. Unlike me, Julie loves to be around lots of people. This job allows Julie to express herself away from me, and I think that is great, as we are so close these days we could quite easily exist without any other human contact. I am already very fussy about who I spend my precious time with. I choose my precious people very carefully. Julie is far more gregarious, but it does make me smile when after thirty years of often-turbulent marriage (is there any other kind?) she says she misses me every day and looks forward to our banks of time together. Recently we exchanged the following e mails – remember we are only a few miles apart.

> Hello, you,
>
> Not sure if you will check your mail before you go to bed.
>
> But am here safe and all ready for another shift.
>
> I know I shouldn't, but miss you.
>
> Sleep tight and see you in the morning
>
> J xx

* * *

Hello you, xx

It really is okay to miss me. Don't let it affect your time spent away from me.

I would say that it is totally normal to miss a guy with whom you have spent over 31 years of your life. I miss you. I guess missing people is like boredom and spending time alone. We need to learn to be aware of the normality of those feelings and embrace them.

When you read this you will have arrived for your last night on this shift pattern. Make sure you enjoy them and don't ever wish them away. Every second is precious, and rushing any of them doesn't give you any more or less at other times.

I will be about just where you left me.

See you pretty soon.

Adam xxx

* * *

Perfect ... Lovely answer and lovely to come into on my last shift ...

Mr Special xx

J xx

* * *

Relationships can be very long, hard and, if you don't learn fast, very unforgiving, but once you choose a partner and invest yourself fully, you simply have to develop and grow together and only quit as a last resort. Work at it. You will be rewarded. Couples need to be expectant of the wicked, devilish, or demonic side as much as the fluffy side of love, and they need to cope with both. Obviously, one side is easier to cope with and the other side most commonly ignored, but there is no relationship without both sides being present. There is no love without adopting the vulnerable position of giving oneself over 100 per cent to the other. Hold back, and I believe you will fail. I know! It's scary just thinking about it.

I look forward to Julie arriving home more now than I did in the first flush of our union over thirty years ago. Possibly an effect of almost losing everything we had and appreciating it more. That is just one example of something in life that money can't buy, and for me it is part of the authentic stuff we should be acquiring – as opposed to the material gains we seem to sacrifice all to achieve before eventually realising that they leave us hollow and blindly searching for that which money cannot buy and never could. I would add that I want stuff as much as the next man but it is just that it no longer rules my life.

 Prophetic Rant

This beautiful autumn morning I walked the dogs and then sat in my garden looking at the surrounding golden trees and listening and seeing the birds flitting from tree to tree. I was struck by the stark contrast with the busy road running close by, and the local airport spewing out planes every few minutes. What struck me most is how oblivious the majority of humanity are to the beauty of our planet and how disconnected most have become. They have their heads up their arses as they strive to accumulate more stuff with little or no realisation that their stuff will be pretty useless when the time comes for them to embrace nothingness. Modern man has lost touch with a vital part of what makes man special, his deep connection to others, the planet, and nature. Science and capitalism have severed the umbilical cord. Modern man is nothing but a hollow shell of former generations. All intuitive and spiritual powers are lost to him. There can be only one end: the destruction of our planet and the breakdown of society as the planet's natural resources are drained by modern man's "success" and absolute greed.

How the hell can working-class man be so short-sighted? I guarantee that the ruling classes have already taken steps to ensure they will survive well past the masses' expiration date. They will not be sharing when the time comes. Much can be done now. In my future thoughts I will cover some of the steps that can be taken to aid our survival. The first step is awareness. Consider yourself aware – I am a bit grumpy and feeling frustrated today. It'll pass.

Role Reversal

I have just fed the dogs for the second time today and prepared dinner for this evening. As well as certain things that have to be done, such as the aforementioned, I have spent most of the day writing and reading. Julie is out for twelve-hour days, pursuing a career which she quite simply loves. I am doing what I love plus trying to make Julie's life just that little bit easier.

A Spouse's Guide:
How to Train your House Husband

This set-up works well. For years I worked every hour of the day and some of the night in various businesses while Julie stayed at home. At times I would be away from home for up to a month at a time. It's fitting that now Julie gets to exercise her independence. I am lucky that the kids have grown and left home. The dogs are challenge enough for me. That would make this end of the arrangement impossible for this man. I am the first to admit I could not do the job Julie did in bringing up the kids from morning till night. I am not sure many men could – although they might say women have it easy. It's not easy at all, just different.

I am in awe of any woman who copes so well with so many different tasks. It's not because she can multitask any better than a man can. We are equal in this. Divided attention means just that for any gender. But rather I admire how she is happy to turn her hand to any task, switching from one to another without hesitation, and never needing to prepare, organise, or analyse. She just gets the job done, whatever it is. That is my experience with Julie. I only hope you are all as lucky. It's time to put the dinner on. Now where did I put that apron?

... and then I told her. "WOMAN, I am the man of this house and what I say goes." Which pretty much sums up how I ended up out here...talking to you.

A late addition to this piece is the information that Julie may be independent but her sense of direction still stinks. Having travelled to the same place for the last week as a passenger, she managed to put in a full tour of the Midlands on her way home today. She got lost – horribly lost.

 Educating Automatons

Just when I think I have heard everything, another situation pops up. My mum, a rich source of happenings for me, told me about a parent of two young children, just school age, so around five and seven years old, who has the central heating come on every night because the kids sometimes wake up cold and uncovered. These are the same kids that have had an iPad for the last three years. I am regularly informed how clever these kids are. I have great difficulty understanding how kids that are supposed to be so clever and advanced have yet to discover how to cover themselves when they get cold. Could it be that they are smarter than their mum when it comes to manipulating her to dance to their tune? I think the answer is yes. Is common-sense parenting, or parenting at all, a lost art that has been replaced by buying lots of stuff to distract and get their love? For me, this is another example of humans becoming more intelligent (maybe) but less able to use reason. I sit here, shaking my head and pulling faces. Finally, I shrug and move on.

Summer Solstice

Summer solstice has arrived, the longest day, and I have postponed my bonfire celebration due to a deluge of rain. My infamous bonfires are made inside, carried outside, and lit. They are made up with boxes and papers saved over the months and built up in the largest box. This produces excellent dry, self-contained fires that are both intense enough and guaranteed to ignite. It's a short, sharp, and efficient way to celebrate. Once the fire is going, any extraneous flammable materials can be added. We are planning to celebrate sometime today. Once again, it's a bit too wet for Julie's naked pagan dancing. I feel summer solstice would be her best chance. Alas, it is not meant to be.

The woods this morning were beautiful. Wind and rain, but not cold at all. The sounds of the wind and rain in the trees combined with the birds in full voice was truly spine tingling – a priceless moment. As usual, and quite amazingly to me, we did not see another human being while we were there. It is great, from a selfish viewpoint, to have all that wondrous beauty to ourselves. Looked at another way, it is extremely sad that with all those chimneys in view, there was not another solitary soul drawn enough to experience nature on his or her doorstep. No doubt they were all too distracted by their techno-gadgets and turbulent lifestyles. Very sad.

It's a weekend morning. We have nothing planned today; it's an Off-button day. We have introduced off-button days when we turn off any technology and fast from it for the day. It does usually accompany a day of fasting. Julie is reading through Book 1 for errors, and I am writing. We will enjoy the two days of twenty-four hour company until Julie returns to work Monday, much the same as other people, with two major exceptions: Zero technology. We still have no television or car, although we do plan to reintroduce both when we feel we are ready for them to enhance our lives as opposed to being dependant on either.

It really is amazing how these two boxes control lives. We are more accustomed to life without their consideration, a richer life for human experience and with so much more face-to-face interaction. This life suddenly thrusts forward after years of diversions and begs to be lived, to be thought about, and to be considered for possibly the first time ever. It's a scary moment, producing more questions than answers. Scary, that is, until you realise you have your whole life to find answers, and yet more questions, and to see how the great thinkers from history looked at this same world. Many of the answers will never be available to human thought. Thought is a limiting factor for humans. However, many eureka moments are still there to be uncovered. Discovering that much of life, one is misled to believe otherwise, in order that the masses be more easily controlled. It wouldn't do to have people thinking for themselves. Let them think the same as others, like a good conformist amongst other good conformists. Rumour has it that freedom is overrated anyway. It is very uncomfortable and lonely to be away from the herd and have to think for yourself.

At 6 p.m. I carry out the bonfire, which I subsequently light. We both sit totally mesmerised and unerringly speechless for us, watching the dance of transforming energies that is fire. I am quite amazed by the deep mental state bought on by staring into the flames. We speak occasionally but on the whole we are hypnotised for around an hour.

I am reminded of another conversation I had with my mum about those same children discussed earlier. She told me they kneel close up to the screen of a huge television in order to supposedly watch the programmes. I am sure that a massive television cannot be viewed at all from that close. I suggested that those children were merely placing themselves in a trance state with the sounds and colours and that a responsible adult should not allow them to continue such behaviour. They are being conditioned by the television and the advertisements.

My bonfire experience just reinforces these views. Once again I am amazed at how little parenting actually goes on these days. I happen to know that this mother spends her time on her notepad, online shopping. It's an addiction that capitalist society stinkers hope the whole of society will suffer from in the near future. I am left once again shaking my head and shrugging as to the lack of common sense or reason exhibited by generations of supposedly well-educated humans. They are educated purely to consume, it would seem. Is our education system lacking the content to educate well-rounded, logical human beings in favour of creating humans conditioned to produce and consume for the economic machine? Is natural human development being overlooked in favour of their training as automatons in a robotic society? I will leave this thought here with these points and hope you join me in refusing to accept all these concerns as normal and harmless. They are not. There is major cause for concern. You need to start waking up and taking care of business at home. Quite simply, you need to start by getting better yourself.

It is quite amusing how Julie and I get all excited about the longest day but still go to bed so early, around 8 p.m. We never actually see it get dark at this time of year but always get up in the dark to catch the sun rising

 ## Big Knit

"Good morning! Only six months to Christmas," was the delivery man's rather strange greeting to my mum as he delivered his parcels. The conversation grew on the same topic, as apparently our happy chappy had already done all of his Christmas shopping. Chirping away, he informed my mum that he had gone out to buy his son a woollen jumper only to discover that it cost £100. Did that faze our intrepid action man? Of course not! He did what any red-blooded male would do in such circumstances, faced with such a dilemma. He went out and bought knitting needles and some wool and knitted the gift instead. A little bizarre? My mum was suitably impressed, being an avid and highly skilled knitter herself. She stated that there was nothing wrong with that and that lots of men knit. I am not sure he thought there was anything wrong with it until my mum placed the thought into his head. I agreed that there would be nothing wrong with a man knitting but did say also that I was not aware of any men who did knit.

My mum then said it was a pleasure to have such a positive delivery driver and that they were normally all complaining about anything and everything. I agreed, laughed, and said that might have something to do with her new friend having escaped from the funny farm. I added that he might be stretching the tale a little. Can you imagine his son's face when he received his first-attempt knitted jumper in place of his £100 designer first choice? Looking at it from the human, non-materialistic angle, the work and love included in the mythological knitted jumper was priceless and totally unique. I just doubt his son would see it that way. It would be a funny moment and infinitely more memorable as a human moment than the run-of-the-mill jumper gifts dished out during the festive season.

It was a gift that could bring people closer. We should celebrate the individuality of our delivery driver. However, I still don't believe it. I love that my mum still has enough faith in people not to doubt him for a second. I need to learn from that example.

 ## Choices

I had recently been preparing for an annual bodybuilding show that I attend each year. I say had because I have now decided not to compete. I am halfway through my preparation and in the best shape of my life. Why? I have been struggling for quite a while about where I would position competitive bodybuilding in my ever-evolving philosophy for life. When one is young, one tends not to have a philosophy for life, or anything else, for that matter. As you mature, a personal ethic becomes important, as do the values you live your life by. I still train and maintain a decent diet all year around. I always will; I do that for myself. The question I asked myself but had no answer for was "Why compete? Why do I need to go on stage to meet others' expectations of how I should look?" I still have no answer that doesn't feature my ego rather too prominently for my liking. I view the inflated ego as a negative. In order to get better, I would ideally like to be less ego-driven. That is the current state of play. I will never compete again, but I will do everything bodybuilders do. I will even be in shape all year around. Most of the guys I know never achieve that. That is my standard for myself. This whole issue is not that clear in my mind even now. I hope to evolve this thought. This will go on until I eventually lose my attachment to my body, my suit of armour that I wrongly feel has protected me through my life.

Possibly the answer lies in the reason I, a basically introverted man, began competing in the first place. Was bodybuilding a subconscious backlash, my psyche balancing the books? There will be more of this as I try to understand. There can be no doubt that wanting to be the best is ego-driven. I didn't compete to be less than the best, although I took defeat rather too well at times. That is because I had improved, and that is all you can ever control, your own improvement.

In hindsight, competing did gain both Julie and I much more respect than if we had never taken to the stage. Did I really do it to gain the respect and admiration of others? Oh dear! It looks that way. I don't like that. It really doesn't sound like me at all. A moment of truth. We all have a little or a lot of that which is considered good or bad within us, I know that much. In fact, I aim to discuss the realisation of my malevolent side quite soon. The secret, if there are any real secrets, is obtaining an acceptance and ultimately good balance as we move through life. Having a personal philosophy is a way of giving meaning to our lives as we progress and start to question our existence.

I can draw a comparison here between the bodybuilding and going public on stage, so to speak, by deciding to attempt to get my writing published and widely read. I feel the difference is that the message in my writing can be delivered with very little boost to my ego. Opinions and thoughts about our planet and other stuff are not special. We all just need to learn to wake up and make some changes linked to those eureka moments. We need to feel that we can all make some tiny difference, and we can. That has to take priority over everything else. Awareness is the only way to combat what goes on behind your back. Then you pass on that awareness to others. The longer Mr Nobody remains Mr Nobody, the better. We can do without Mr Nobody becoming Mr Somebody and losing the message in a celebrity fog of no significance. We need substance to prevail over style, just for once, in the twenty-first century. Is that even possible?

 Plants

For some strange reason, I have a house full of thriving plants. Cut flowers expected to last for a week will live for three or four weeks in my house. My mum, a self-confessed plant expert, can't believe how plants seem to love being at my house. The house is small, and the plants are so successful they dominate. Some are too big, but I don't want to let them go anywhere else. I joke with my mum that we have good energy in our house. I say joke, but I do actually believe that there are more positive and less positive energies all over the planet and that humans go a long way to creating their own. Maybe merely having that belief is a good starting point. Julie, Holly, Jake, Smudge, I, and any visitors must create a nice place to be for plants and flowers.

Our house is rarely turbulent. After a very turbulent past I wouldn't tolerate that. Any turbulence is restricted to inside my head; outside is nice and calm. I do actually love and appreciate plants and flowers. They boost my moods, so I guess if being in a place that calmly appreciates your existence creates the perfect environment, this is that place. Plants are not objects to me; they live, they are not fixed, and they change. I am not sure how I feel about cutting flowers; I would rather they were still attached to a life source. That may sound quirky or like some more of that craziness, but that is how I feel. And yes, I do have the odd one-sided conversation with my plants, more a case of me flattering them for their beauty than discussing any real heavy politics. I'm telling the truth. Waking up from a meditation confronted with an array of fantastic plants is awe inspiring. It may even be that plants hate the poison oozing from televisions, human noise, and turbulence, and they are our too-much-turbulence barometers. This could be an early warning sign that your high-tech gadgets and noisy, distracted lifestyles disconnect you from nature – or, alternatively, that you are getting it right and life is boosted by being in your house. That means all life, including your own.

 ## Narrow-Minded Beliefs

I am always wary when talking about religion, as there is no more sensitive subject or topic where rational thought can be overruled by faith. Thus a seemingly logical argument will come up against a stubborn resistance, based on no obvious rational thought process. I have two, maybe three, small thoughts on religion today. My first thought is this: Could the desire for an intrinsic, intuitive knowing of something named God – in whatever form we wish to visualise it, from a man-type figure right through to pure energy – actually be a human drive? Do we have a God drive? How else could the durability of such diverse beliefs be explained? God exists in one way, shape, or form because our human instincts tell us it (or he)

does. Religion is built into our subconscious. It is our task to work out the details for ourselves, or just be comfortable in not knowing the details.

Keeping an open mind is key but currently the belief I like is that God is an essence, an energy, and part of a totality including the whole of nature. That makes God for me indescribable. I also believe that science, mostly via physics, plus instinct is the path to unearthing as much as we need to believe comfortably. We will never know. For most humans, blind faith is too much to ask and can disguise the fact that the belief is just not valid. Some intellectual and spiritual pointers are needed. For me, that is the case. My current beliefs are based on some strong instinctual feelings and some science that could be argued to back up the possibility of those same beliefs. It just makes more sense to me than any other path. My God is everywhere, constantly, and will live on through that same energy that cannot be destroyed. I am, however, very willing to accept any logical progression to my beliefs. That makes God an archetype created from psychic energy and fits very well with Jungian theory.

The ridiculous nature of many of the orthodox beliefs also makes it easier to find a more logical path. The path predates Christianity by 5,000 years. It's a path that evidence would show led to Christianity via plagiarism and lies. On this path, the stories told are intended to be allegorical, not literal or historical, as Christianity has manufactured them in order to control the vulgar masses. My biggest fear is that orthodox religions have never been much more than tools for social control, with very little room for truth. Christianity would be so much richer for the acceptance of that fact that it is the hidden meaning and not a manufactured reality that holds the riches. At the same time, leaders should trust that the vulgar masses are not as stupid as they believe, and they can come to terms with allegorical material and grow accordingly.

Finally, I would say that the search for a true belief system would never end, as much like human's evolution and development, it is a lifetime venture and voyage towards new pointers and new beliefs. I find it hard to accept that anyone can fix their beliefs and close off their minds. Narrow-mindedness is the scourge of the human race, as I told a lady who knocked on my door to sell me her religion in the way she had set in her mind. I suggested that rather than knock on people's doors, she should spend the time reading and developing her beliefs, in order that she not be left in the dark ages. She was not amused and informed me that she was doing what Jesus had done. I informed her that the Egyptian Iusu had allegedly done it also, 5,000 years earlier, and it might be worth her exploring the possibilities her Christianity offered her in the twenty-first century. I hope she doesn't meet the same fate as her archetypal hero.

As you can tell, I am not great with people trying to exert their opinions on others. This lady was ignorant of any belief other than her own fixed opinions, which were not even her own but rather others' opinions that she has adopted. It would seem sensible to at least keep an open mind to the fact that all things change and develop, either a little or a lot, including beliefs and ideas. Plant the seed and, if it is a good seed, it will grow. Maybe that is the point: the seed the lady was attempting to sow is no longer strong enough to grow without being forced or fed to the weak. But it can be, with an open mind and a willingness to change the way one thinks. I do realise that when it comes to religion and beliefs, many people spend their lives being offended. I sincerely hope I haven' stepped on anyone's toes with my thoughts here, but the nature of thought and change is exactly this process. Listen to what others have to say, let your on-board computer sort the information out for you, and then form your own unique perspective. Moreover, and above all else, never close your mind to any new ideas and thoughts – or, for that matter, old ideas that have been suppressed – when they would serve us well in the here and now. Read, listen, and observe. Your particular truth may even be out there already. Have fun searching. That is living. Therein lies the buzz. It is no coincidence that I am following this thought with the next.

Courageous Thinking

Many people choose not to think and just accept what is suggested or put before them as public opinion. Why might this be the case? Inclinations to avoid thinking exist aplenty. But thinking is our basic means of survival, and we must choose to think. We possess free will. If we choose to think for ourselves and come up against facts we are not prepared for or cannot handle, how do we deal with that? The conclusions from our thinking could disturb the routines of our lives. Thinking may lead us away from the mainstream thought of others, a lonely place to be. Our thinking may highlight personal traits that we do not like. Our thinking may lead us to see things we do not wish to see or previously hidden truths that are hurtful, particularly in significant others. You will see as you read on that I have had exactly these experiences in my life after making the choice to think and analyse.

IF YOU'RE
THINKING
LIKE
EVERYONE
ELSE, THEN
YOU AREN'T
THINKING.

www.marcandangel.com

It is understandable that we wish to avoid any thinking that causes pain and discomfort. The choice to think is genuinely courageous, and in many cases the choice to continue on that path after experiencing the painful and frustrating consequences of original thought can be termed heroic; that's no exaggeration. Awareness through our thought process can produce a view of our world that actively seeking unawareness can protect us from. The attitude is "What I don't know can't hurt me." A pathological condition, such as narcissism, may even develop when the individual does not relate to anything outside of himself – a common condition amongst twenty-first-century humans. I can't go back to a life of blissful ignorance. Besides, it would no longer be blissful, as I now know I have the choice to think. I doubt I could stop now.

In deciding to be more aware through thinking, we are not promised success. We are free to try without any guarantees. My experience is that there is rough and smooth. There is far less comfort and more frustration once we make the decision to open up our awareness through thought. Everybody would be happy to be aware and thinking if there were a promise of success; with a guarantee, fewer would opt for the safety and comfort of conformism. The uncertainty over leaving the herd and becoming an individual, free in both thought and action, is built into the very essence of our existence. A level of anxiety is normal and needs to be accepted as such. The feeling of being a square peg in a society full of round holes is how I would explain my life away from the herd thus far. The feeling here is one of incompatibility. I am the square peg.

Many of you may be saying that everybody thinks all of the time and wondering what the big deal is about thinking. You fully believe that all of your choices are your own and that you are free in every way. The fact is that most of the human race is conditioned from birth to live what the existentialists call an inauthentic life as part of the herd. This is one choice, and it is comfortable. Many do not ever get to realise that there is another choice. This is called, unsurprisingly, authentic living. This is when, for whatever reason, normally an increase in knowledge, one becomes aware that there are other choices.

The more natural mode of being for a human is to exist as one among many, not to opt for a path of self-realisation or tough self-examination. But this is living inauthentically. The alternative is to throw ourselves into drawing our own conclusions about what is real or true, separate from public opinion and conditioning. Awareness is the only solution to combat what goes on behind your back, coupled with a refusal to accept as self-evident the things that are proposed to you, and an eager and interested attitude to explore and to know.

To emphasise the point of just how tough it can be to go against public opinion and conformist thought (or non-thought), many former so-called communist states ran programmes of re-education for those who did not conform to new social norms. Free and original thinking was simply not allowed. In a democratic society, it is a matter of where the limitations are placed between a need for social control and the freedom of each of us to think and believe as we wish. Humans have a natural disposition to impose their will on others, either by rulers or by their fellow subjects and public opinion. This tends to erode individual freedom and increase governmental power.

In my limited time of attempting to master the art of individuality, my awakening as such, I have found the biggest initial strain to be on my family and significant others. It can seem at times that they really are robots, as they repeat and reinforce universal opinions and behaviours. All conformist views become so much clearer and at times are almost laughable to me as they are delivered one after the other. I am finding that I have to be guarded and not challenge them every time. These previously went unnoticed by me, as I held similar mass opinions and had no point of reference with which to dispute the conditioned truths. The big issue is that they do not have access to anything but the media that instils these beliefs. I have been introduced to other ways of thinking via my reading. Often, in exasperation, I suggest reading a book. They are too busy staring at screens and consuming more stuff ever to entertain that idea. We seem to have become separate species of human beings.

167

There is hope, though, as I find there are people who are attracted to a certain point of view; they have not seen any alternative to the norm before, but they may now be ripe for awakening or interested in there being more to life. They often listen and are intrigued by points of view different than the accepted norm. This is how freedom begins, and often there is no way back, as Jean-Paul Sartre famously wrote: "We are condemned to be free."

 Birthday Suit

One of the magical moments guaranteed to bring a smile to even the grumpiest face is that moment when a toddler gets the opportunity and some free space to run around totally naked, giggling like a crazy thing. They just love being naked. I wonder then: Why do we condition all of that uninhibited joy out of developing human beings? We can learn so much from kids before they are fully conditioned for social control. Giggling uncontrollably seems to be lost in many humans, and not giving a jot about being seen naked by others is also very rare. That's probably because you would be arrested for indecent exposure. The word indecent when used in connection with our bodies speaks volumes. Why is the human body indecent? Years of conditioning.

168

When did we learn that the human body is something to be ashamed of? We are told it is indecent and that anything but the ideally shaped body is unacceptable. These beliefs are deeply ingrained in our developing psyches, so much so that many of you will be cringing to think of being seen naked or giggling. Heaven forbid one would run around naked, giggling, whilst the authorities chased you to cover you up.

Never dance naked because the body has parts that do not stop moving when the music stops!

"Streaking" is frowned upon. Streaking is the label that the supposedly unnatural behaviour has been given by the media, and it is not shown on television for fear that it may encourage more of the same. We are losing the authentically natural behaviour, that fantastic, uninhibited impulse we first witness in toddlers. Let's have more streaking, and not just babies! Next time your toddler streaks around the room or garden, why not join him? It might just loosen you up a bit for the day ahead. Toddler streaking will then become just one less of the many repressed urges that Freud saw as corrupting our natural human impulses. You are going to condition your kids out of something that gives so much joy. And what could be more natural? This thought does help to make one aware of how much parents have become part of the conditioning programme for social control, the process of turning humans into consuming robots. The process quashes individuality for being far too inconvenient. There are no special cases. Everybody has to fit into the appropriate categories and exhibit normal behaviour. No difference is allowed. Fancy a streak, anyone? I don't think the urge ever really vanishes, particularly in those who are in touch with their inner child.

Every time I discuss with Julie a pagan ritual to celebrate, her first question is, "Can I dance around naked this time?" I always reply that she can dance naked in the garden whenever she wants. No need for a planned ritual; if it feels good, do it. Julie is in touch with her inner child. I envy her for that. I try, but my conditioning is strong. How repressed are you? I am not condoning running around everywhere naked; that may get you in trouble, but I am encouraging you to be aware of the conditioning process we undergo and to fight becoming that society robot that is so valued and comfortable for society and unfulfilling for the robot himself. Is that really living? That is the big question. At some point in our lives, we all have to face the decision whether to fight to break free or settle for comfort in conformity.

Age Again

I am led to pondering on how a child must begin to formulate an idea of ugliness in older people. When we are talking here about old in a child's eyes, we may only be discussing adults in their mid-twenties. Physically for a child an adult has enormous size, they would seem rigid and movements would seem awkward, maybe even jerky and unpredictable. With rough, wrinkled skin, large ears and noses and relaxed eye lids, added to either natural yellowish teeth or in America and increasingly in Britain and across the world an unnatural glaring white mouthful of fake ivory snarling down at them.

Besides being fresh and unmarked itself, the child has impossibly exacting standards when it comes to their skin, teeth and complexion. Then the aroma of choking perfumes and deodorants or sweat, tobacco or beer. The possibilities of the effect of smells are almost infinite and surprisingly enduring as we age. Part of the ugliness can be that faces rarely look good from below which is the perspective from which a child views their world. Having briefly touched upon sight and smell, adding the other senses can take the

171

experience to horror proportions. Imagine happily playing when all of a sudden a giant, smelly face from above ambushes you, swinging you into the air and mashing either a whiskered or made up face against your soft skin. At the same time screaming like a banshee and inadvertently spitting in your face. Then passes you roughly (playfully) to the next monster to repeat the experience.

There are no seven wonders of the world in the eyes of a child. There are seven million.

We all still remember the relative that insisted on that behaviour as a norm. You can see how that could either result in years of therapy, an aversion to older people or at the very least a nervous twitch when sensing the signs of an imminent geriatric ambush. Viewing them as an entirely separate species until you actually reach the same point in your life and through that eureka moment develop some sort of understanding that provides the belated meaning to the more stressful moments of your developing years. If you are lucky you will simply erase the memory of adults from your young mind and at the same time from your meaningful world. However, you may just grow up viewing those strange adults as the enemy, your dictating rulers. An ugly species that you need to break free from in order to find your identity. All joking aside it is worth remembering how incredibly distorted is the child's vision of the world. And how we should all approach the responsibility of young people with some calmness and dignity.

Random Creativity

I would like to share that, to me, the feeling of being creative, once discovered, is like a drug. The need to create becomes a part of me. The only way to survive without it would be to allow myself to be constantly distracted by the gadgets and brainless pastimes society supplies so plentifully in order to gain profit from my distraction. The problem I have found personally is that, no matter how much I try to plan my creative moments, creativity appears to act randomly. Eureka moments arrive when the environment is right, and that right environment can be almost any situation. Sadly, it's often when I have no means readily available to create. Maybe it is ludicrous expecting creativity to strike just when I am ready.

Learning to be less rigid and less organised has been difficult. For me, awareness and sensitivity to moments of creativity, those eureka moments, has proved therapeutic and has taught me to stay tuned in to myself, the moment, and the others I am with at that time. At the same time, I am learning the skill of relaxing and letting ideas percolate and surface when the time is right. I view my brain as a kind of sorting station. I enter data by all the quality methods available to me, such as reading and intelligent conversation. My brain sorts the data and allows me to continue with the intelligent conversations, understand the reading more each day, and write creatively, relating all of the above to my particular and unique experience of this life journey.

The most important time is now, and the most important person is the one you are with now. This philosophy, applied to our every moment, would indeed allow for full participation and minimum distraction. I am becoming more aware of the growing list of petty distractions that take over our lives if we allow it. They include compulsive consumerism, internal chatterboxes, driving everywhere, fast- and slow-food outlets, fast and slow casual sex, idle gossiping, television, mobile phones, social networking sites, hundreds of so-called friends, and a multitude of gadgets with bright lights and wacky sounds, to name just a few. They lead to hollow people. The barrage is constant, and the desire for profit will never abate. I battle each and every day to gain back some meaningful time. Quality reading, quality conversation, nature time, silence, intense exercise, and quality-over-quantity relationships all go to reset the balance for me. I still lapse, but I now know how to battle the distractions. I have weapons at my disposal. I am taking my life back while I still know how to live without the distractions and while those weapons are still available, before the world is full of hollow people. The world is full of beautiful people but they are just having a nap.

 As Nature Intended

I have on my wall two inexpensive prints of paintings by Van Gogh. Both are paintings of tired and worn looking footwear, boots to be precise. I love these prints as the condition of the boots sets the imagination alight on what may have been the history and background of the boots whilst included in the lives of whoever had worn them. They have an amazingly interesting and lived in quality that invites my imagination to run riot as I look at them. Boots that could so easily have been extras in a D.H. Lawrence or Charles Dickens novel. Every picture tells a story.

I find myself comparing the boots to an aging human face. Full of life and experience. Full of emotions, both sadness and joy. Now take a moment to compare this face full of life to the society ideal face of the 21st century. Often chosen from a catalogue. Wrinkles surgically removed, whitened teeth filling the mouth space and hair dyed. Maybe even injected with poison to remove any trace of having lived a life or indeed experienced any emotions. Communicating absolutely nothing. I suppose the shoes could be judged similarly. New shoes often cast aside before they are able to show any proof of a history of a life lived. Not even made to last. Are human beings becoming objects or more to the point how many human beings have allowed themselves to become objects already? Why do we fear the beauty of aging? Are we so afraid of death that getting closer actually repulses us? It is obvious that many humans treat their corporeal being as just more stuff. To be updated should

175

or when it begins to show any sign of a history or experiences. What I would simply call character. I ask again why we fear the beauty of aging. I have been intending for some time to combine two images side by side in a picture frame. The first image would be of a plastic faced, fake toothed 21st century robot ideal, possible a television presenter as they seem to care what people think more than most. The women seem to be under more pressure than the men. Men can be very average looking to be featured on television whereas women seem to have to be young and glamorous by the standards laid out by a shallow society through various mediums.

An expressionless catalogue selected designer face that is more a testament to consumption and profit than to any life lived. All beaming and complimentary to other such fake personalities, creating a need in any person watching to look the same. To never become old. It never works and just looks ridiculous I feel. My second image for the picture frame would be a human being aging as I believe all human beings should age. A face telling a story, a face that springs to life with a smile. A face accepting of the aging process as an integral part of the human life cycle. A face with a story to tell and nothing to hide, nobody to impress. Picture these images side by side. What story does each convey? One is a mystery to be unfurled by one's imagination or face to face communication. The other a product of the modern age. A material asset, bought and paid for and thus owned by the human but at what expense? A face the same more than different to many others. Sadly, a face becoming increasingly sought after and acceptable as a way to increase status with others. The natural face, the natural aging process is increasingly denigrated. Getting older is becoming something that disgusts and terrifies many young humans. This will be the case as long as there is a profit in attempting to hold back the years with no effort. There is no profit in the aging process and always profit to be found in situations of fear by making false promises and creating illusory, joyful and fake futures in the consumer's head. The individual can make a stand and if enough do then the profit will dry up and more people can just be themselves without feeling it a sin not to want to change or be something other than you are. I am enthralled by boots or faces that inspire the imagination, not by faces or boots that are difficult to identify from computer generated images. It looks from my viewpoint that rather than computer generated image creators striving for their creations to look more human, many human beings seem to be wanting to look more like computer generated images. How long before we can't tell the difference or have a percentage of the population reached that point already? I would argue that human beings that eat well and exercise are already perfect in their myriad of imperfections. The facts are – we are born – we age – and we eventually die. Let us at least do that with some dignity. That includes living with the physical appearance of human beings and not a computer generated human likeness. An idea likely to change with the wind for more profit. How long before one updates one's face and body the same way as other material possessions? " I can't be seen in the same face as last year, what will people think?" Already happening? Yes, in certain social circles.

Boots and faces to be lived in and last. I want to see faces that I can read, faces that contain some left over humanity. Faces that prompt me to want to know of their history, their struggles and their victories. A face befitting a life well lived. I want to think the words "I bet that face has some tales to tell." The same way I look Van Gogh's boots and know there is life contained within.

 Gadget Self – A Blind Alley to Happiness

I heard about a very good way of appraising whether a piece of technology has real value for the human race or whether it should never be allowed to exist. If the technology enhances the human organism it gets the thumbs up but otherwise it is useless or even destructive. There are many current technological staples that would fail that test. The problem may not be the technology but rather the overuse of it and the greed from the companies to bleed every last bit of profit from their product. The automobile may well go down in history as one of the primary factors in the destruction of planet earth. How many car owners' really need such a big car or need to use their cars as much as they do? But are too unwilling to change their lives, even for the sake of the future of the planet. I wonder at the sanity as I walk down the road of many cars per household parked all over the sidewalk/pavement so pedestrians have to walk in the road to pass. That used to be against the law but somehow it gets ignored by the authorities these days. As the profit from car sales is paramount to the greed of the 21st century. I see many Mothers having a rhino stopping truck to get their kids to school when it is just around the corner. We have no rhinos in this country and most of the offenders would benefit from the extra exercise out in the fresh air. There is not a person alive that would not benefit from more exercise.

Gadget self buys every gadget available at the expense of their humanity. More machine than human. Technology is great. The abuse of technology is a threat to our freedom and to the planet. It is a very fine line that most of the human race crosses without a thought to how it is changing who they are and how they evolve in future generations. These behaviours become the norm via mind viruses called memes and change the evolution of the human race. On the plus these memes can be positive also. We can make better choices and spread viruses that will save the planet or we can continue down the path of greed and more suffering and ultimately bleed this beautiful planet dry. Think about the technology that will really enhance your human potential and not what the greedy profit mongers tell you will bring you bliss. Bliss together with any human emotion worth feeling can only be found inside of yourself and that promise is a downright lie. Your purchase gives you a boost for a short time and then you are back looking for the next gadget that will really make you happy this time. How is that working out for you? They lie to you constantly. How do you feel about that? Still feel like lining their pockets? Buddhism makes it simple here – The secret is to want what you have and not want what you don't have.

I clearly see five of the seven deadly sins in gadget self. At a stretch I could include all of the sins but I don't clearly see anger or lust but the rest are all present and thought of as totally normal behaviour. Gadget self is normally covetous (craving), envious, gluttonous, prideful and prone to sloth. A lovely picture. A Frankenstein creation of the marketing man. One that he can sell to until his heart is content and his bank balance is bulging. Finally replacing him or her with the next generation of automaton, conformist consumers. Incidentally, it is easy to think that I hate technology. I don't but I do hate the belief that it is all good and the mindless and obsessive use. There is middle ground to be found. The goldilocks "just right" moment. When technology and man work in perfect harmony and we are not even close to finding that middle ground. Primarily because nobody is looking for it.

 Having It All

Today, the four points of the compass will be full of stressed, irritated and at times even aggressive people all working toward that perfect life that will come tomorrow and if not tomorrow then very soon. What will give them that? A bigger house, new car, expensive jewellery or maybe even a holiday. It hasn't happened as yet, they have forgotten the last holiday, night out, new car, crazy diet, the last exercise fad or new electronic gadget but the next one will be the one that makes them truly happy, brings them joy. Maybe it will happen and maybe they will chase after lasting happiness in material possessions and fake promises for their entire life.

Materialism is more than just wanting to accumulate the biggest pile of stuff, bigger than all others, before you die. The goals of consumer culture are striving for money and possessions and having the right image and being well known socially. To be achieved by capitalism and consumption, much of it conspicuous, so that everybody can see how cool we are. All connected in a search for a sense of worth outside of oneself and desiring the praise of others. Seeking satisfaction extrinsically from money, the ideal look or from the admiration of others. For the materialistic self the ultimate purpose in life is to attain financial success, social recognition and an appealing appearance above all else. No real surprise here, as that is exactly what is being sold as the perfect life by any company wanting to make profit. Research indicates that adults who focused on money, image and fame had less meaning in their lives, less vitality and suffered from more depression. Just to make matters worse for these aspiring social icons they also reported more headaches, backaches, sore muscles and sore throats than their less materialistic counterparts. This was consistent for men and women. Materialistic individuals also had more narcissistic tendencies which is in keeping with the widely held belief that our capitalist consumer society is a production line for narcissistic personalities.

The issue it would seem is distinguishing between a simple wanting and a genuine psychological need. A need is not just something a person wants or desires but is felt necessary to survival, growth and optimal functioning. Needs direct our behaviour in ways that increase the likelihood of those needs being satisfied. Psychological needs require fulfilment for psychological growth to occur.

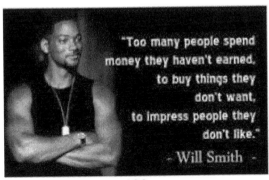

"Too many people spend money they haven't earned, to buy things they don't want, to impress people they don't like."

– Will Smith –

You probably can see yourself here either a little or a lot. For our society to prosper there needs to be millions of hopeless consumer selves buying things they don't need in order to find a happiness that never or only fleetingly arrives. I know the drive is inside of me to buy. I have grown up conditioned to be greedy just like the rest of the western world. I know I want many things that I don't need. But I am aware and I am getting to know myself. I can't be beaten now. I am awake. I know I will still buy useless stuff but I only need to compare my consumption with others to see I am getting much better. The difference? I have accepted the addiction, problem or attachment and I will continue to get better until I am back fully in control. I don't accept that just because everyone else is behaving the same, it is considered normal and as such it is right. Normal greed is still a very sad sight to behold, and when you see it in yourself the affect can be life changing. There are very few people in the western world that will not witness greed in themselves if they look with honest eyes. Hiding behind the fact that they are in the majority. My tip here for anyone is to watch others in any shopping area and see how obsessive and greedy they look as they fill their bags with stuff that they need to make them happier and better than others. Fighting for deals at sales time. Losing all dignity in an outrageous show of greed and hostility. Hear the conversations of justification as to why they need each item. Then know that a short while after getting home with the booty there arrives a flat feeling. The desire has gone and the mood was only temporary. Just like a child at Xmas after the initial obscene glut of frenzied and blind present opening. Now what? Not the child's fault and the parents did manage to make the child happy for a short while. Now what? That empty feeling always comes along. Alone with ourselves. That is what we need to learn to love. Ultimately the buzz is in the desire, the pure fantasy built around that desire, reinforced by the marketing and sales team promising emotional benefits and even endless joy. The reality of what is desired is too boring for words but nevertheless that is the reality. You are built up just to be let down from a great height and you still can't manage to get a little pissed off at the inhuman way this is knowingly perpetrated on you and your loved ones. If you think shopping online is in anyway less of a problem. Think again! It may feel more civilised and dignified but all of the same greed and desires are driving your behaviour. Yes, of course you need everything that you purchase. The same way the alcoholic needs another drink just for medicinal purposes. Online shopping is even more dangerous. Like a solitary drinker at home. When you are alone, nobody is there to judge and you can quite happily tell yourself good feeling stories to justify your habit. We are masters at telling the stories that retrospectively explain our actions as rational and normal. That is how we do it. We live life forward and narrate it backwards so it matches, or appears to match in hindsight our plan (of course we had one) and intentions perfectly. Truth is we are scrambling around in the dark and there is nothing logical about most of our choices or behaviours until we at least wake up to who we are and how we act, not as is the case for most of us how we think we act and who we imagine we are. What is misleading about the state of mind of the members of a society is the widely held naïve belief that if the majority of people share certain ideas, feelings or behaviours that this then proves the validity of these same ideas, feelings and beliefs. Nothing could be further from the truth. The fact that millions share the same vices does not make them virtues. The fact that millions share the same errors does not make them truths and taking it a logical step further the fact that millions share the same mental compulsion does not make the people right minded. There are many instances throughout history that prove that the majority are often very misguided.

I want to finish this section with a thought that often crosses my mind. A purely fictitious scenario but maybe not so far off becoming a reality should fuel run dangerously low on the planet or some other such possibility or should that be probability. Possibly more a matter of when than if. I want you all to think about this from an individual, personal point of view. How you are psychologically set up for the following situation? How attached are you to stuff in your life and how much of you is left if all the rest is removed for even a short while? Let's say for four weeks you lose the use of everything in the list below. With these main avenues of escape closed what would be the consequence for people thrown back on their own resources. How dependant are you on stuff? There is nothing wrong with anything on the list when used to enhance an already fantastic life. However, it is too often used to create a fantastic life and the human organism withers and dies behind the stuff.

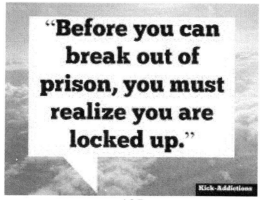

"Before you can break out of prison, you must realize you are locked up."

Kick-Addictions

185

Most of my friends wouldn't get past the first thing on the list so don't feel too badly. Feel challenged to keep in your life only what enhances your humanity. This may be the toughest challenge of all in rediscovering your true self. Losing attachments and desires. I wonder is it possible to have all of the following in one's life and yet not be hopelessly attached to many of them. I am sure in just four weeks there would be nervous breakdowns and anxiety attacks. I wonder also if the powers that be, whoever they are, know that humans can't survive with themselves and much of what capitalist society produces is there to stabilise our delicate psyche and keep us occupied. I wonder where they will be when the planets resources run low and we can no longer be amused and temporarily satiated by their high priced toys and gadgets?

Four weeks without attachment to the things on the list below – I have forgotten many more but the following are a selection of our attachments and addictions, just of the top of my head – even if we do not readily agree to the terms attachments and addictions, it is difficult to argue if we can't live without anything outside of ourselves. Are we in control or are we being controlled, often with our blessing. An automaton existence.

- Mobile phone

- Any motorised transport

- Television

- The internet

- Take away food

- Snacks and soft drinks of any kind

- Shopping for anything other than moderate food needs

- Alcohol

- Recreational drugs

- Newspapers

- Movies

- Idol gossip. Fine to talk about ideas.

- Computer games

- Talk radio

- Sports events

- Social media sites (no internet anyway)

- Gambling of any kind

- Sex

- Body Image

As you can see and maybe get the feel for the lacking of the items on this list. As you think more the consequences become even greater. It is definitely worth thinking about. How those thoughts develop for you and where they lead you in your life is all part of the exciting adventure. Or you will shrug and continue to consume and look for happiness in that list. There is always a choice. I have eradicated much of the list from my life as obsession. I think if we are to live with others and not on a mountain top there has to be a gradual process and a regaining of control from this inanimate list of stuff. I was pleasantly surprised how well I have done by taking my addictions and attachments one step at a time. I actually feel I need to learn to use some of the list to enhance my life, such as Social media sites. Which is why I am here and you are reading this. It is easy to control by abstaining from such sites but the art in growing myself is to get over my fears and use these valuable resources to enhance my already good life.

I acknowledge that I have an obsessive personality and as such I can get carried away by most things. Shopping is a constant war for me. One in which I have made vast steps forward but still buy some crazy shit that I will never need. I will get there. For me on that list I need to venture into the internet more to enhance my life experience whilst staying in firm control and I have accepted that shopping will always be my Achilles heel. I am conditioned to shop, we all are, but I am getting better. Getting better is why we are all here on this planet. All of the other items on the list, I have no attachment to at all. I am attached to reading, writing, exercise, the dogs and Julie. I appreciate that the reading and writing are nevertheless attachments and I tolerate them as I feel that I grow from the experience and that I can help others through reading and writing. I have detached myself from my exercise or at least my identity which I will explain later in detail. That was a case of realising I am more than a body but also a realisation that the body is one of the greatest gifts we will ever receive. A balance of body and mind is required. One of those cases of creating a new perspective on the situation. Shining a light from a different angle.

I agree that I am coming from an extreme angle but left to flow with society we will almost certainly become its slaves (if we are not already). What is needed is some drive in the opposite direction and to settle when we have it Goldilocks, "just right". That does not happen without much work on getting to know ourselves and controlling the subtle dominant powers exerted on us by society in favour of a more balanced psyche. Finding the contentment, we seek, not in stuff outside of ourselves but rather inside of us where it has been waiting peacefully for recognition all along.

 Been There, Done That, Got The T Shirt Self

This is not the same as the "know it all" self as this self always admits to knowing nothing but always knows someone or a source that is an expert on absolutely everything. There is not one single topic of conversation you can broach that they will not hijack with either their expert version of what you are saying or any subject loosely related. I have one of these in my life and I never get the opportunity to speak for long. I even have to sit and listen to what someone on the bus says that overturns a thought that I may have inadvertently let pass through my mind and let slip out of my mouth.

Been there–
done that. Then,
been there
several more
times, because
apparently I
never learn.

There is normally a favourite "go to" source that reigns for a while. A person that has made an impression on this person. The reign is normally very short lived. The source can be anyone, the postman, a builder that has done work recently, the lady on the bus, the lady on the bus's son or an acquaintance, a magazine, a book, a newspaper, the television, the internet, any expert that is placed in front of this person is speaking the absolute truth. I am guessing that when away from me I become one of her experts to flout in front of others. Although I can't for the life of me actually remember getting the opportunity to impart any wisdom. I have learnt to sit quietly and just let her run on her own. She has little need for me in the conversation. This identity is ripe for social control. I am amazed how much capacity this woman has for filling her brain with details that are useless. The simplest point in a conversation can take an eternity to say. Something that can be imparted in seconds has to be prepared for meticulously and delivered with not one detail left to chance. I often have relatively important topics of conversation regarding family that are left unsaid while I listen to what I can only describe as hours of worthless rubbish. She then has the cheek to say that I don't tell her anything. It is impossible to tell her anything. As far as I can see she already knows every single thing that has ever occurred in the known world. I know I sound as if I must be exaggerating but if you know such a person you will know that this is real and one of the wonders of the world. A real test for any budding seekers spiritual growth. I do feel decidedly unspiritual even writing this section. To make the point I have often said that I do not want to hear about certain people's turbulent lives in conversation (gossip) and even as I am saying that she can't shut up from talking about the very person I am fed up with hearing about.

YOU TALK SO MUCH SHIT

I DON'T KNOW WHETHER TO OFFER YOU A BREATH MINT OR TOILET PAPER

I hate gossip. The pain in her face when faced with having to not speak is a sight to behold. The scary thing is that we all have a little or lot of these identities in us all. I wish we all had the ability to see ourselves as others see us just for a fleeting moment. Psychologists would say the reason that certain types of identity grate on me is because I am looking at myself within the other. I am projecting my psyche onto others. I am actually seeing myself and I am not liking what I am seeing so I get rid of it on to another person. A case of "I don't want this trait, here you can have it". If that is the case! Ooer! I'm in trouble. I have noticed this before with other people and following a conscious effort on my part to discover why I am so bothered I have managed to deal with the issue in myself and the whole thing just disappears from my external life because I have dealt with it in the only place that I can, inside of myself. Isn't it fun to realise how we go about burying ourselves under layers of identity that we can't even recognise as the fake selves we have erroneously constructed to survive. We are a very complicated species. A worthy project for life. If we are honest with getting to know ourselves we should be able to see all of the selves I am writing about within our own psyches, either a little or a lot. Food for thought. I know I talk too much and it is on my list. My very long list.

 There Are No Ordinary Moments

Saying Yes to Life may start with saying yes to your groceries.

I have inadvertently discovered as good method of testing whether I am able to accept "what is". A method of checking if I am ready and able to say yes to life.

I am in charge of organising the home delivery of our grocery shop, more or less on a weekly basis. I make the choice to accept substitutions for any items not available when delivery is due for whatever reason. I could mark "no substitutions" but I choose not to. Originally and still at times now I gripe about some of the insane (to my mind) items that are seen as fit substitutions. I became aware that I really get disproportionally bent out of shape about the smallest changes. I remember at one time being very angry that I moaned at the guys delivering, they are helpless and as such are innocent and I was so far out of order. I couldn't stop myself, I was totally out of control over groceries. I apologised and after they had left I sat and reflected on why I was so annoyed at something so trivial. That is a story for another time. What I needed now was a plan to grow from my grocery shop. Yeah, I know a radical concept but we can progress from anywhere.

I have learned over a number of weeks to shrug and accept whatever is sent, finding a positive in every choice. It has been touch and go a couple of times and I have caught myself in grumpy flow more than once. But I am getting better.

Why all the fuss about the shopping, is it really that important? Yes it is and here is why.

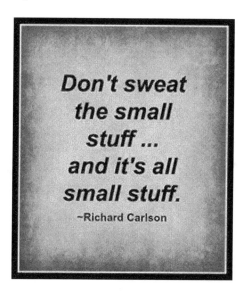

Don't sweat the small stuff ... and it's all small stuff.
~Richard Carlson

I figure if I can't accept and say yes to supermarket substitutions, I will have no chance when life's bigger surprises enter my life. My online grocery shopping has become the training ground for a bigger and better attitude to life and as such a springboard for personal progress on a much larger scale. Reminding me that there are no ordinary moments. Life will go on wonderfully in spite of the hardship of my having to accept plain bagels as a substitute for cinnamon and raisin bagels. It does sound funny when I type it. I wonder how often we get bent out of shape about stuff that seems ridiculous in hindsight? Too much! Is my guess. Accepting what we can't change is a big step in releasing ourselves from needless stress.

Life is crammed with substitutions apart from our great expectations on a daily basis. We never really know what we are going to get even if we do build up our expectations to fantasy levels at times. With this in mind it does pay to flow with the seemingly unpredictable nature of life.

A small side bar to this piece is that one never can predict where our life lessons are going to emerge from or in what form our teachers will appear. However, emerge they will and if we hope to progress throughout life we must remain mindful and tuned in for these learning experiences. They hardly ever come nicely labelled for us to identify when to attend to the moment. Life winners are ultimately life's best learners. Look for those hidden lessons. Your life will be crammed full of them.

 Heaven On Earth

Here I stand at sunrise, on a postage stamp of woodland on the edge of Luton, some of Mother Nature's best work. To the east is

Hitchin, a bustling town. To the north lies Luton Airport, where planes are rumbling. To the south, a busy dual carriageway connects Luton to Hitchin and produces white noise twenty-four hours a day. So much for the eastern corridor. Finally, to the west is Luton, a noisy, traffic-congested town. One guarantee is that the four points of this compass will be full of stressed, irritated, and at times even aggressive people, all working toward that perfect life that will come tomorrow, and if not tomorrow, then very soon. What will give them that? A bigger house, new car, expensive jewellery, or maybe even a holiday. It hasn't happened as yet. They have forgotten the last holiday, night out, new car, or new electronic gadget, but the next one will be the one that makes them truly happy! Maybe it will happen, or maybe they will chase after lasting happiness in material possessions for their entire lives.

I come to this oasis every day at dawn with Julie, Smudge, Jake and Zing, my three terriers, four if you include Julie. Do I come here to think? God, no! I come here to try not to think but just to enjoy. My chatterbox is going all day and most of the night, usually talking total rubbish inside my head. My dawn walks are purely about being present in this precious moment. I focus on now. Listening to the birds, in awe of the trees, and even at times spotting deer, I watch the sunrise and enjoy my dogs just being dogs. If we see people, they are always happy and friendly. Mother Nature brings out the best in us all. This is my moment to practise the "being" part of human being. Together with a daily meditation, this is when I understand the meaning of heaven on earth, or at least inside of me at these moments.

It hasn't been easy to slow myself down for these moments, and at times my yappy chatterbox still wins, but when he shuts up, the knock-on effect for the rest of the day is well worth it. No drugs, no alcohol, and no expense – just a little time and a different perspective on life is all that is required. You don't even have to have the dogs. They are most definitely optional, but for me they are the icing on Mother Nature's underrated cake. Find the mind's off button, and feel the pleasure.

 In Praise of Walking

I was about to leave for my walk to the gym when a friend, who was leaving after a fleeting visit, good-heartedly offered to take me in her car. There was a confused look on her face as I pointed out that if I went in her car I would be deprived of the exercise, appreciation of my senses, thinking time, fresh air, the chance of real human contact, birdsong, the elements, and all else that might eventually be included in my walking adventure, which I deemed a blessing. I should probably include the chances of death on a pedestrian crossing, as people do not seem to stop at crossings these days. It must be fashionable to mow down pedestrians and so inconvenient for motorists to stop, as the law states.

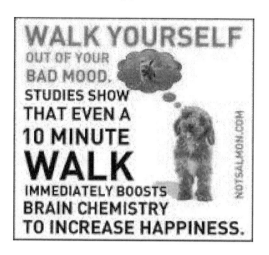

If she walked with me, I told her, she would experience all of the aforementioned, benefit from my scintillating company enroute, save fuel, and benefit the planet. She now looked even more confused than before and declined my invitation. I think it was because I was going to the gym, and she may have an aversion to gyms. I am pretty sure she mumbled idiot under her breath.

 Computer Generated Ideals

A picture in the newspaper of a jacket on the thinnest model I have ever seen. Actually that is a lie they are all that shape. Knowing that these models become the ideal for millions of young girls when will the people involved be forced to depict a more varied ideal. I am not saying skinny is not OK but I am saying when that is all that one sees it becomes an ideal and the fact is all women are uniquely different and any newspaper or magazine should have a responsibility that their overall message is just that. They should be able to utter "over the course of a week, our paper or magazine contains all the shapes and sizes women are inclined to be during their lifespan". Is that not good sense? And stop messing with the pictures. Computer enhancement means that young girls are aspiring to be cyborgs. They are trying to achieve the impossible. Perfectly shaped, blemish free perfection. Keep it real. Keep it human. Warts and all.

 Choices

If you are playing Russian roulette, there is a right choice and a wrong choice. The wrong choice gets your brains blown out. Choices are rarely as simple as that, the simplest of choices with the direst of consequences. When making choices it would seem that one often assumes there is a right choice and a wrong choice. If the choice made doesn't work out as predicted, and to be fair how could it realistically? That is predicting the future and is rarely accurate. Then the chooser decides they have made the wrong choice assuming for some reason that they know how the other choice would have worked out. And it would have been better than the choice made. The possibility of either both choices being disastrous or both being perfect never seems to fit the psyche of the chooser. One is the right choice and the other is the wrong choice. One can see how this would lead a person to procrastinate. Looking for the right choice rather than just choosing the most likely suitable option and then getting on with the consequences. As for regretting the choice made, that is never a wise move. The other choice may have been better or worse, but more importantly one can never know and as such regretting the unknown is simply ridiculous. When the choice is made the other choice ceases to exist and should be regarded in this manner. There will be plenty more choices for you to think about in the future without dwelling on choices that never existed once you had made your original choice. Choose wisely and then move on to future choices. Your choice now is do I know what he is talking about or do I need to read this again? Will I regret it if I read it again? No, you made the choice, live with it. Time to choose.

 What If? Thinking Out Loud

Death is so totally a part of the life, death and rebirth scenario throughout nature with no exceptions. Life and death are contained in every moment. Our bodies are living and dying constantly. What we see when we look at each other is more dead than alive. This is the natural way of living things. The paradox of every opposite being contained in the other.

 **A Thought!**

Surely our moment known as death would also contain rebirth. Why would we be the only exception to the rule? Our bodies die but we are reborn (psyche) to keep progressing. Otherwise all that we have become for better or worse would be lost under a time limitation and humanity would stagnate and regress.

I don't accept there is a use it or lose it angle to wisdom gained throughout our lives. Rebirth would mean a higher starting point and as such progression. What if all of our subconscious knowing is our accumulated experiences and gained wisdom for our current and future use. We know this stuff because we have always known, we have learned it all previously. It would make total sense that our accumulated life wisdom from our psyches enduring existence would be available if we are able and wise enough to access it, by mastering our humanity. We know because we have always known and have become too distracted to access our wisdom which appears to us only fleetingly and surprises us when it does.

Unless you are more connected such as Einstein or Jung who experience more of the collective wisdom than most. We are probably all as gifted but have been so heavily conditioned that we fail to see with any consistent clarity. We have precious moments that slip away behind the barrier of our conditioning all too soon. Leaving us with a sense of "knowing" we are more but unable to unravel the mystery. We have lost the keys to our inner universe.

One doesn't have to read too much to know that we have so much untapped potential. If only we could shed the prison that is our cultural and biological conditioning by pressing the "restore factory settings" button. Although we would then lose the useful part of that conditioning. Doubtless there is much we have gained from our enculturation. What we require is an alignment of psyche and our cultural personalities (ego), including our shadow in order to progress to becoming whole. We would see with such clarity.

I am convinced although still contain doubt which keeps my mind wide open, that those small magic moments of insight and coincidence hint at what is possible if we can get free by loosening the grip of our ego and harmonising with our psyches. We are all imprisoned away from our true natures. Our Cultural personality, shadow and psyche yearn to be "just right".

At this point in time we have hopelessly fragmented psyches. Our first part of life civilising process creates that state in us. Separation is the order of our external world and our inner world. Our task in the second-part of our lives is to bring it all back together again and unify our psyches and once again connect to all there is. If survival is the mantra for the first part of life, then wholeness is the mantra for the second part of life.

Being whole is not possible on a mountain or at a retreat it has to be all or nothing. We are social, by aligning ourselves we align others.

The odds are stacked against this truth but maybe that is the challenge for mankind.

The big question must be for the human race – What comes first, extinction, realisation or maybe even evolution to a higher consciousness?

The race is on and it is only through progressing ourselves that we may make up the lost ground, find the true meaning in our lives, and save Gaia and all that she nourishes. Every speck of life and death is included, we are all in this together, and linked until extinction do us part. All of life is one. One amazing progressive process that we are all so lucky to share. With this book I am suggesting that we all progress together from Soul2Whole.

Flexible Labels

We are all guilty of attaching labels to ourselves and others. Look at how you label yourself upon first meeting another in the flesh and in your cyber world. One of the first questions we ask of another is what they do, so we can compartmentalise them in our heads according to our less than unique or real perception of their role. We all have pre- (ill) conceived notions of a person based on the very few words they use to identify themselves.

I awoke having thoughts about how the labels given to us by others and the labels we like to assume only serve to limit our potential. I have always resisted labels knowing that once labelled it is very difficult for others to see past the assumed label. The power of suggestion is a powerful and mysterious force and labels often suggest a finished product, that we call self. This self may at first seem like the person we have always dreamed of being but once attained and abstracted by others it can seem very limiting. We are masters at underestimating and undervaluing our capabilities and labelling ourselves accordingly. It is better that we aim high and strive than aim low and succeed.

Think hard before you limit yourself, keep moving and changing so nobody can affix a label. By exploring and discovering your unique talents no label will ever seem right. There are no labels for the authentic soul–self that we all contain buried deep within, often under assumed labels.

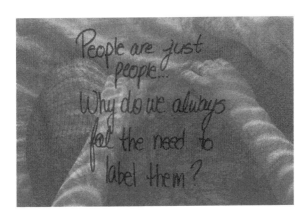

In a nutshell, rather than becoming your label, assuming the noun. Replace the noun with a verb and engage with the verb. This for me would entail that rather than "I am" an author, progress therapist and motivational speaker that I engage with writing and helping others by using the tools of speaking and therapies of differing kinds. These talents can then be added to past talents and any new discoveries can be added as we progress.

This makes life a mystery participatory process with a mind wide open to new possibilities. There will be no answer for the question as to who "I am" but much to talk about under the banner of what "I do". "I am" is a subject of much greater depth and possibly the task of a lifetime for each of us to discover rather than dismissing it by hiding so much under small labels that can never define the largeness that is an authentic self.

 ## Know Thyself

The reason we spend most of our time distracted with gadgets and rushing around is that we have a morbid fear of having to spend time alone with ourselves. Being quiet in a room alone with our thoughts is a situation that many humans avoid from the time they wake until the time they finally sleep again. The golden age of communication makes this easy. We never need be alone.

It is never easy to discipline oneself to work from home. This is something I have constantly been aware of and struggled with. At times I feel as if I am just keeping my head above water. I have managed, but should you ever take the opportunity to create from home, never make the mistake of thinking that it will be easy. It may well be the hardest adaptation I have ever had to make. Julie tried it once and lasted less than two weeks. Humans hate boredom; they do not like being alone constantly, and unless you are organised, you will fail. You will spend long hours doing nothing and failing to apply yourself. You will feel worthless and unproductive, and the mind games will begin. You will begin to question your whole existence.

This last few weeks I have noticed a disturbing change in many areas of my life. I now have to work too hard to discipline myself to walk the dogs, a job that I normally love. Reading is a chore, as is going to the gym. All of these would be top of my list of things I love to do. I have been a regular gym user for so many years and compete in bodybuilding shows. Now my reading is irregular and not at all concentrated. I am even deterred by the weather when planning walks. That is simply unheard of. I have begun to fall asleep when I am reading. I am constantly re-planning my workout and diet schedule in an attempt to re-motivate myself and make up for missed sessions and poor nutrition. To top it all off, I have not written a word for over a week. This behaviour is most unlike me.

This last week I periodically planned new starts in all of the above but seemed to fall at the first hurdle – not even a hurdle. All of the aforementioned are areas of comparative expertise for me. They are better accomplished without too much thought. Am I thinking too much? I am writing this by hand in the hope that the reflection might kick-start my more normal behaviour patterns. Some who know me might say that my current behaviour is more normal, and I am too disciplined generally, and I expect too much from myself. "Give yourself a break," they would say. They would probably encourage me to eat more junk food and be lazy more often. That is not who I am. For my life to work for me, I have to rely on self-discipline. It feels good. I must discipline myself to discover my seemingly effortless drive for the important areas of my life. The drive is anything but effortless. Looks can be deceiving.

As I handwrite this, the dogs are asleep next to me, having been walked by Julie alone this morning. The time for the gym has just passed. My laptop with current project screaming out for words is asleep, and my eating has been less good than usual. I sit thinking, which area attracts me the most to move my arse to change? I decide it is my writing, as I am already handwriting my journal. Surely it is only a few short steps from the couch to my desk. Where to start? It matters not, as long as I start somewhere. I have lists of topics. The first words are always the hardest to formulate. They need to come without conscious thought. Nothing comes. Am I afraid? Maybe, as I am nearly finished this book, and then my newest work will be available for others to judge. I am amazed how much I have changed over the course of a few books.

I have always thought that if you search hard enough there is an opportunity to get better in every experience. Writing my journal informally whilst away from my desk is my re-discovered treasure in this instance. I have developed the habit of writing directly onto my laptop computer or pc and in the process I have neglected a very productive and therapeutic set of writer's tools. The rediscovered tools are a pen, paper, and the flexibility to write anywhere, in any mood, either with or without a lap.

It could be that, for me, sitting at a desk at an allotted time and ordering myself to think and reflect is the problem here. The position I am reclining in allows me to be part of my room, relaxing with Smudge and Jake, blue skies and birds visible from the window. The position allows me to look at my many plants and just take time to enjoy my surroundings between thoughts. It allows Smudge to lean against me, which she seems to love to do, I assume for security. Maybe I just needed a change.

I have come to the earth-shattering conclusion that both modes of writing are crucial to the process. A handwritten method can be used wherever I deem something worthy to be remembered and hopefully a lesson learned. And the work can be finished on my laptop, at which time even more reflection will have taken place (maybe) after the event, thus enhancing and expanding the thought for the finish.

Amazingly, once I began writing about a lack of motivation and discipline as an issue, I continued this piece and become aware of a total change in my attitude and motivation as I am writing. Julie says I am quirky. I have rediscovered an old friend, my journal. I am already planning events we will attend together. In the space of possibly 500 handwritten words, I have turned from pessimistic to exceedingly optimistic. Maybe Julie is right – that does seem particularly quirky. I had forgotten how much pleasure I get from writing my journal by hand anytime and anywhere. I recommend journal-writing to others constantly. When did I lose the habit?

It's a timely reminder and also a lesson on how easily one can lose certain habits that are so low cost and rewarding, yet capable of unlocking the door to your very soul if you can just allow yourself to cut loose. Journal-writing has always been so liberating for me. I care not who reads my journal. I have never really understood how protective some people can become about having their feelings shared. Your journal may well end up as the only place your authentic self can exist in our fake role-playing society of the twenty-first century. It may help you stay in touch with who you really are, if only for yourself. Keep a journal. It will be time well spent away from television and those exceedingly antisocial social networks.

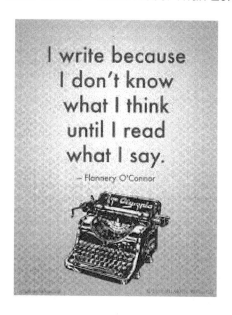

I write because
I don't know
what I think
until I read
what I say.

— Flannery O'Connor

What about the other areas of my life? I had stopped being a writer at the gym or when out walking. I had stopped observing and reflecting. I had temporarily lost the curious part of myself that questions and analyses everything, the part that is never bored and always inquisitive. The part that sees a worthy tale in every walk, every encounter, and every gym session. The natural world, the unnatural world, and other people are all that I need as a writer. How strange that I lost my way with something that appears so naturally a part of me. Perplexing.

I will share two texts that I sent to Julie at this time, to give an idea of my struggle.

Text 1

> *Took the hounds. Back door open for them to bugger about.*
> *I needed the walk too. Very strange mood I am in. Creative*
> *Adam fighting to get out but mind too unfocused to produce*

anything but big ideas with little or no substance. I am sure this won't be permanent, and at least I am aware so I can fight and analyse it. It's not happening behind my back without my knowledge, and being gadget-free I have nowhere to hide. In my position of having to discipline myself, it does make life feel meaningless. I am achieving nothing. All I have is my training to conform to and any routine I can force upon myself. I have nowhere I have to be, no commitments except to myself. Maybe while I am like this I should get out with the dogs more often and train every day to give myself some structure. We saw Sunday the state of me if I stay in. All I did was sleep. A useless lump. Too much time and no motivation for anything. I need a relatively uncreative routine for this period. Just simple to follow without feeling redundant. Very strange, because I have so much I need to do but just can't get going.

Julie's Reply

I can see you have been struggling big-time. X. Getting out with those two is always a good mood enhancer, bless them. X. The writing will always be there and come back to you. X. Easy for me to say. But you just have to ride it out. and eventually all will be perfect. X

Text 2

Maybe getting to know myself that little bit better. I am sure I have taken the right path but had no clue how hard it would be to get on with myself. A challenge millions subconsciously choose to avoid their whole life. It would be more comfortable to conform and hide. Not now, though, because I know better and a tougher but more liveable life awaits. This feeling is part of the life struggle for an individual in our times. I had gone soft over the years, relying too much on distractions rather than face up to myself.

What this thought has depicted is man's (not just me) struggle with freedom and an inability to be able to spend time alone quietly. Man conforms and distracts himself in order that he never has to confront his authentic human self. Jean-Paul Sartre stated that man was condemned to be free, and Erich Fromm highlighted man's fear of freedom in his book of the same name. What I experience are the symptoms and feelings that manifest as the inherent anxiety of a free man. Man is in a unique position of having separated from nature but as yet not having fully attained the destiny prescribed for the success of his own species. History should tell the tale of man's journey to his ultimate future, if he is to be a success. It's an ending that he may never reach, as it would appear man has lost sight of his destiny. Man's goals are widely accepted as being the total harmony between man and nature and between man and man. I think one could add between man and himself.

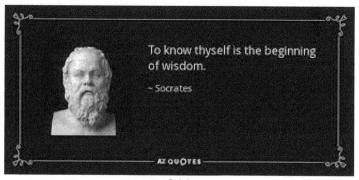

Maybe that is the place for each one of us as individuals to begin, by getting to know and becoming comfortable with ourselves minus technology and distractions and then using both sensibly to enhance human experience. Nobody said life was supposed to be easy. Get better. I doubt anybody ever really gets to know themselves as we are such complicated organisms and wear so many masks it is almost impossible to know where the real self is hiding.

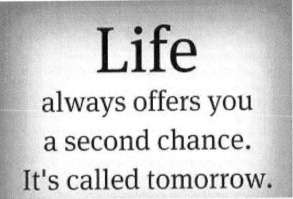

Life
always offers you a second chance.
It's called tomorrow.

http://TheFunnyPlace.net

 Just Say It

This morning I had a moment when I thought Julie might be feeling taken her for granted. I always act on those thoughts. No blame, no excuses, no regrets. I never want to be wishing I'd had said words when I had the opportunity to say anything I like, anything I feel. When I am settled down to writing is when I am struck by this stuff. My brain is affected by my desk and chair. My thoughts flow freely and as randomly as is possible. Am I crazy? I think we are all a little unique, crazy, and insane, and the more individual you are, the crazier you will appear. I am totally all right with people thinking I am crazy. It's a small price to pay for my freedom. The point is not to regret missing any opportunity to tell a loved one how you feel. I have tried that and the second chances are few and far between in our short lives. But there is always tomorrow to start that new life.

Email is the convenient media for instant personal communication. I never put anything I have to say off for later, as often later either doesn't come or thoughts just plain float out of my head until the next time I am in the zone, in my bubble. This morning's slushy moment follows.

> *"I suppose you are as close to being my perfect woman as it is possible to be. Spot on, in fact. Over 50 years old, with a great body and never using age as an excuse. You spend your life always being close to your inner child, and that is something that I envy you for. We are the same in many respects. In other ways, we complement each other. My Mr Sensible keeps you from being a total nut job, and your inner child keeps me smiling and aware of mine. I do a pretty good Mr Nut job. Sometimes I get so frustrated at the way the world and humanity are heading I forget to live my life. I feel as though I have to do something. In reality, I need you to ground me and just keep me doing what I do. I will write until the day I die. There will be a lot of words. I hope they can make a difference one day. I would love the power to be able to physically shake the whole of humanity, just to get them to wake up and to make them aware; then they could choose the best for themselves. Most humans are never given all of the facts. Frustration is a negative emotion and in*

this world an emotion that could be the death of anyone caring too much. It is probably already shortening my life. You had better make me laugh some more to get those years back. You are so rarely down. The magic of a smile as you age is that it reduces age in an instant. A special moment that plastic surgery and Botox users are robbed of experiencing. A human moment. I have never wanted a wrinkle-free plastic partner, just a partner that cares enough about herself to always be good for her age and never to stop improving who she wants to be both inside and out. Or putting it differently, to be the best that she can be. Never listening to what others, society, or media labels tell her she should be. Aging together with you is an attractive proposition for me. I fancy you more than any woman I ever see. You are unique. There is much of me in you. The years have conditioned me. I am trying to be the best that I can be. Inside and out. I hope you see what I am trying to become. I see you. You are what I need, even the silly, slightly annoying bits teach me not to overreact.

Did you find your phone? It wouldn't be you unless there was a question such as that needing to be asked. You need to attach your phone to your person. At times I feel like your father. It works for us but never without hard work and a lot of mutual understanding of the other. We are each part of the others' education and development. A part that has some great perks, by the way."

Catch you later.

Adam, X

Putting Yourself First

Is it better to be part of a team, an individual, or can you be both? After the very excited period of getting everybody in a group, come what may, as they were supposed to work better that way, a psychologist, probably the same one that extolled the virtues of group work, decided that keeping everybody apart and working on a problem provided far more solutions and more originality than the group situation. No surprise there really as most humans in a group situation just loaf about or adopt others opinions. Being alone forces one to come up with one's own ideas, thoughts and input. Maybe then an organised group discussion can take place. There are times when I despair as I see society as one big group where there are a few original members but the majority are happy to go along with the flow of the majority even if it is obvious that there are other more worthy options to be considered. The infamous and much favoured in society herd mentality, a favourite of mine. For me the answer is that individuals must develop themselves for the entirety of their lives and come together as a group of individuals and not as members of a herd. If, as that individual you no longer fit the herd. Good for you. At least you will be free and not locked up in others opinions and ideas. By others I include all media, politicians and even the gossips. Any place that somebody is telling you how and what to think. Nobody has that right but it happens the moment you are born. Start to notice. If you feel locked into the system I would suggest that you start to read away from the mainstream literature and discover the other ideas and options available to you. There are reasons oppressive regimes over the course of history burn books as a hostile act. The reason is so you will not be able to read doctrines other than those you are expected to believe in. We are all at any one time being controlled. How much or how little you are aware of this is up to you. I know that I like to know at least some of what is going on in the real world. And that means turning the crap off that is on the television. Soap operas are not real. Heck! The news is probably not even real or at least not without extreme bias towards whatever regime controls it. The truth may not even be out there but you might get closer than you are getting currently from the media.

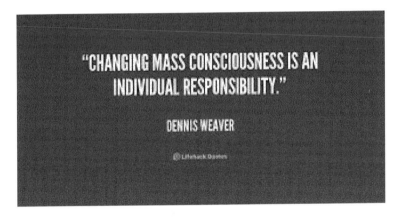

It is often said that individual philosophy is selfish and that living in society it is egotistical to concentrate on developing yourself as an individual at the expense of the group or society. The point is here, that you are not looking to develop at the expense of the group. The best version of who you are, should, and will be, better for all that know you. If that is not the case then it is the group that is probably narrow minded and reduced to an object and therefore wholly unworthy of your support and continued allegiance. The selfishness here is not with the individual. Can there be a more selfish example of human behaviour than clicky groups getting together for whatever noble cause and distancing themselves from others whose beliefs do not match their own. These groups, and they number many and get together for all sorts of reasons, from friends and family to religious and political groups, allow their social conditioning and downloaded beliefs to lock them up. They are locked away and closed off to other ideas or behaviours other than their own learned behaviours. There is a saying " birds of a feather flock together", true, but for me that should not be viewed as a good thing in a multicultural, multiracial society one needs to be able to mix and understand to some extent others very different lives. Ignorance and labelling has only ever been a breeding ground for hostility. Individual development is about remaining open minded to all the many differences others find to segregate themselves from others. And thrusting oneself in amongst those uncomfortable differences. Once again difference is therefore celebrated and approached with a curious and compassionate hunger to learn and grow. An awareness that we are forever becoming until our eventual demise. Upon death is the only time that we become an unchanging object relative to our current human understanding of what may or may not come next. When faced with new difference in others we all have the tendency to retreat back to the comfort of our own herds. That was the case for my encounter with the man in his dressing gown and slippers on my morning walk. He was behaving different and I wanted to run away, I just needed to feel comfortable. How laughable is that? I will act differently next time. More curiosity and less searching for comfort. Thinking about the situation now, I wander how I will ever discover anything new without at least a small amount of curiosity and a lot more bravery. That can probably be said for all of us. I consider myself an individual before a group player. If I have to work so hard to stay free think how tough it will be for some of you that are firmly entrenched in your various herds to break free in even a small way. Start with having opinions of your own. That is not meant as an insult but rather, it isn't until we start really becoming aware that we realise we are adopting others or general society opinions. Often we do not even think there are different points of view until we begin to delve into our real choices. Start by reading some books that are never in the book charts. Once you begin to read there flows a reasonably natural progression. Leading you from book to book. Most good books will either reference or lead by subject to where your curiosity will take you naturally. Don't fear any topic, they all have something to enable us to learn and grow. Maybe even go for the books that create that fear inside of you due to a subject you are resisting. For example, the word God or money seem to illicit strong reactions one way or the other. I used to resist the word God. Once I realised it is the idea that I had inherited about God that I feared I set about making my own mind up about God and many other subjects that I had preconceived notions about due to conditioning. Above all, be prepared to contradict yourself on an almost day to day basis. Thoughts and ideas are living evolving entities and one has to let them become in relation to our view of this world. A view that will change daily. It is indeed a fantastic voyage. A spine tingling adventure. Never fear doubt as doubt is what keeps your mind open to new knowledge and different ways of seeing your world. Doubt is a gift to help keep minds wide open to the unlimited possibilities that always appear sooner or later.

Don't Hold Back

Could the secret to committing to living a full life be to let go of fear and just give as much of yourself as possible to all of life's situations? A life philosophy of "Don't hold back" might be just the thing. Include your soul in all of your life.

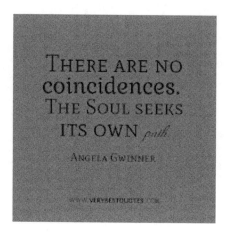

THERE ARE NO coincidences. THE SOUL SEEKS ITS OWN *path*

ANGELA GWINNER

WWW.VERYBESTQUOTES.COM

Not Alone

There are times when one is passionate about life and the meaning of our human existence, times when it can seem from my very narrow-minded viewpoint that nobody cares and we are all basically doomed. As long as others get their stuff and live life distracted, they can seem to care little about anything. There is collective apathy. However, this morning I got into a varied conversation with four other men of ages ranging from twenty-five to fifty-eight years. What a breath of fresh air it was to discover that each cared about, and had thoughts on, the various subjects we chatted about. They were all aware of how they were affected by the topics we discussed. As long as we have intelligent, open-minded, free thinkers and listeners on this planet, there is hope for the future of mankind. From my perspective, it was an amazingly motivating morning. I wonder how large the leap from initial awareness to making small changes is for the comfortable twenty-first century conformist. Time will reveal all, and I hope we have enough of that precious jewel. We need awareness to spread like wildfire in the wind. Ordinary people can change the world.

 Unique Experience

Julie and I were on our way to exercise at 6.30 a.m. before we both began our separate work days. It was a beautiful sunny June morning. On the roads, rush hour, which in the twenty-first century cities goes on for at least four hours, was in full swing. As we sauntered along, taking in the beautiful morning and chatting about this and that, something caught my attention and demanded my total focus. High in the trees across the busy road, there was a bird neither of us had ever seen before. It is always a special moment when you see something for the very first time. I had no clue as to our new friend's label, and I really didn't care. It was a pleasure welcoming the newcomer into our life experience. We watched it until eventually it disappeared from our immediate view. I once again became aware that I was standing next to rush-hour traffic, surrounded by literally hundreds of people who had paid thousands of pounds for the unique experience that the metal box of their choosing would give them or add to their lives. Ironically, it seemed that the only two people having a unique experience were Julie and I, with our cheap training shoes, rucksacks, and God-given human senses. Incidentally, both Julie and I feel we are using our senses better and are more attuned to nature since we have been out walking more. We are more focused and less distracted. We are becoming increasingly attuned to our natural environment.

 Soul Hugs

I'm assuming that human bodies do contain psychic energy; this has been measured scientifically. It is possible to feel that inner energy once you believe and connect to it. Try your hands first. Close your eyes and focus on feeling the energy inside of your hands, arms and then move all around your body, feeling what I would describe as a tingling sensation that varies from mild almost to a buzz. Mine is more intense outside in nature during meditation or just sitting alone with no distractions.

With that energy in mind, how important does that make simple gestures such as hugging a loved one? I call it a soul hug and try to feel the moment with my inner body; apparently my hugging ability is in demand. The hug allows the opportunity to acquaint oneself with both the person you are hugging and your own inner body. It's the perfect opportunity to feel the oneness of all and to realise how much you are the same despite outward appearances. Writing here now, my body is tingling in anticipation, not impatience, of that soul hug with Julie. It will have to wait for today. I wonder if I can give Julie a remote soul hug that she will feel 100 miles away in Birmingham? Quantum physics would say that it is very possible and that if dogs can sense their owners' thoughts and actions when apart, then why not humans? I would hazard a guess that it's because we are more distracted than dogs and considerably more disconnected from our true natures. Nevertheless, I just sent Julie a hug. I have to start somewhere.

All we need is belief in miracles being possible, along with a lot less ego and fewer beliefs that limit our true potential. A miracle is just something that we don't understand as yet. Are we so arrogant that we think we have answers for everything before we experience it? There are many accepted norms that were once believed to be impossible: the four-minute mile, the ten-second 100 m, going to the moon. To early man, fire would have been a miracle. These are just a few that popped into my head. There is no such thing as a fact. The mind boggles as to what we might be capable of if we were to lose our limiting beliefs and know that everything is possible. We need to lose the interference and receive the signal to allow the universal source to flow through us. At the very least, we must learn how to be true to humanity. We are virtually drowning in life potential just waiting for us to learn how to swim and navigate to safety. This entails more than thinking outside the box; this is believing in the impossible becoming possible. Reading books can guide you to what may already be possible but not available to mainstream belief systems. Read factual books and stimulate your imagination as to what is out there. Start to reprogram yourself.

Thought of giving you a hug...
Two hands seem too less for someone like You...
So, here is a jumbo hug...
Keep smiling and have a great day!

I do know I miss opportunities to soul hug. Julie was here for plenty of time, and she is very huggable to me. I was too busy in my head, obviously. That will change. My priorities were wrong. The feeling of missing something only surfaced after she had left. Or more likely I had been unconscious before she left and only regained consciousness after she left. I was not present enough when she was here; that's a situation that blights the human race. My mental note is to be more present for Julie and others and never take anyone for granted. I will have to change my programming and delete some existing programmes that are not serving me well so this can become my normal behaviour, but I will get there. I believe that. I aim to supersede much of my automatic programming and reprogram myself for joy in the twenty-first century and beyond.

Soul Hug: A union of psychic love energies that connects souls.

 Detached

In keeping with my gradual attempts to become as fully human as possible, I am trying to break free of limiting beliefs and attachments that stop me from becoming. Becoming is my term for my being a different person on a daily basis, either a little or a lot. Getting better is all part of becoming; the destination is a total mystery and something to reflect on happily. The odds are stacked against breaking free of the conditioned-from-birth and fur-lined shackles of the twenty-first century automaton, but I like a challenge. With this in mind, I have made the decision to cut my weight training down for a while to only one full body session per week. Until I no longer feel any withdrawal from the attachment. I will still be walking in excess of 5 miles per day in nature with my dogs. I have done this to reduce my attachment to my body. I am attempting to detach myself from being dependent on people, objects (stuff), and habits as much as possible.

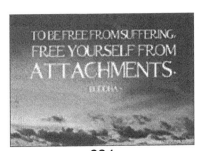

My body is my body; it is not who I am. I do this not to become an isolated hermit but rather to avoid basing my identity on dependency. I want to free myself as much as possible from ego-driven dependencies and distractions in order to produce a more authentic set of relationships with the world around me. My goal is to reduce the ego and unify myself with my world by eliminating any behaviour that produces separation. To this end, by the end of this month I will be phoneless. This is a big step, even for a man that seldom uses a phone. Again none of this is supposed to be permanent, but rather until I can guarantee that the gym or a telephone will enhance my life as opposed to becoming attached to such external fixes. I fully imagine that even a television and a car will be used to enhance my life at some time in the future, but that is a little premature right now.

Another act has been for Julie and me to do more stuff independently. This has been difficult, which just goes to prove how we depend on each other. When I am without Julie, others ask where she is. The same occurs with my dogs. Julie and my dogs are definitely part of who I am, a part of my identity. They form a part of me that I feel uncomfortable without. I will learn to feel comfortable without them in order to love them and not be dependent on them for my identity. I still have work to do to detach myself fully from a rather turbulent past, which I have begun to do quite recently. I have noticed good results in that I feel less resentment for Julie and I no longer feel angry as often, as has been the case for the last ten years, at least. I am letting go, and it works – not overnight, but it does work. Along with this, I no longer project into the future based on that turbulent past, and hopefully we will stop repeating the endless cycle that hanging onto the past and projecting into the future has periodically produced in our lives.

We are breaking the cycle. It has begun, but we are fully aware that our egos are always ready to take us back to square one of resentment, anger, and pride if we do not continue to let go until the past has lost all power to possess us. Ego takes offence far too easily; it is as if every little thing is regarded as a threat to our survival. In fact, that is exactly what the ego is doing, but twenty-first century man no longer needs that level of protection, and love is impossible unless man is willing to let go of his ego. Without love, the planet and mankind are doomed. Am I being overly dramatic? No! Look at human history, and watch the news. Is that a sane race? Looked at without the rose-coloured glasses and without the politicians' spin, the human race is just plain crazy. We're a race of hopelessly out-of-control egos, which we can all bring under control by simply getting better and aiming to reach our full human potential, and this, according to recent quantum physics and other writings, is a potential that we can only marvel at in awe. Our potential is the stuff fairy tales and fantasy are made of.

Impudence

I have noticed something quite worrying about myself. When a person is full of their own self-importance, I react internally. It is great to have self-esteem, but when a person's self-esteem turns into self-worship and placing himself on a pedestal to be idolised, I feel the need to humble that person and bring him back to planet earth. I never act on the feeling. On the other side of the coin – and there are always two sides to every coin – when a person is humble, submissive, and unassuming, I feel the need to boost him or her up. I would say I act in order to do this. But what a cheek! How unreasonable it is of me to challenge others' opinions of themselves. I have done this without much deliberation until now. I will be more mindful and less impudent in the future.

THE ONLY WAY TO SUCCEED IS TO NOT WORRY ABOUT WHAT ANYONE ELSE IS DOING

Every Moment a New Start

How does one even begin to conclude a book on one's efforts to get better by reading, writing, thinking, and acting? The word conclusion means the end or finish of something, the summing up of an argument or text or the setting of an agreement. A judgement may be made after reasoning or a proposition reached from given premises. Books, and in fact thoughts and ideas in general, never really end; they are open-ended. More often they are a beginning for new pathways and fresh ways of looking at all kinds of situations. Thinking only ends when life ends, and we are not even sure about that. Even that sentence promotes new thoughts. So, in keeping with my desire for global open-mindedness, this conclusion is an introduction to a life of reflection, a life spent getting better through reading, writing, thinking, and making small changes. Until the next time our paths cross, I will leave you by saying that if enough individuals work toward harmony with nature, their fellow man, and most importantly, the self, it must eventually make a difference within the human collective, within the herd. The aim is to change the aims of humanity to those same aims, the only reasonable aims for the future. The aims are for unity and harmony between man and man, man and nature, and man with himself. We can each make small changes. Millions of small changes means significant change. Our planet, fellow men, and humanity's future need significant change. We all need to simply work at getting better as individuals away from the influence of the herd. We need to have faith in ourselves as a minority with influence. We must believe we can make a difference by taming our overdeveloped egos.

Beginning this project, I couldn't spot the ego self in the text. By the end, ego self stood out in bold relief. I have made progress, indeed. When attempting to reduce the ego, I have noted that the self changes almost daily. Many of the thoughts and ideas I have shared, I am already seeing quite differently. I am a different person for shedding at least some of my disguises and false beliefs. I have a long way to go. What might the future hold? I am now carless, without a television, and my phone has been dispensed with. I have retired from bodybuilding for now, as I can't seem to place the sport in a life philosophy that does not encourage dependence on anything, including the body. My ideal scenario is to place all that I love in a life philosophy that works perfectly. Seeing life as a journey of endless discovery is a great way to live. I have the curiosity of a child and the excitement of knowing that, thanks to the discoveries of quantum physics and spiritual teachings throughout the ages, there are many possible futures to be experienced. But nothing is certain and probably never will be.

I am writing my next book and already many of the thoughts I like have changed and evolved. In proofing reading this many of my thoughts have changed. I am certainly more accepting and less militant. I shrug more nowadays and am finding a place for all that I love in my life without addictions or attachments. My purpose is to perfect a system that will develop the mind, body, and soul to attain the perfection all humans possess.

There is one thing for sure: Human beings are capable of much more than they currently realise and will never reach full human potential as long as they are buried under a mountain of false thoughts, technology, and distractions.

The solution to all of the above, for sanity's sake, is a nice big soul shrug. Let it all go and fill yourself with empathy and compassion for everything and everybody. It's a gargantuan task that sounds all very easy. The goal is for love and peace to conquer all. Change yourself, and the world will change.

I am now a little less dazed and confused. But do need to find a foot hold in the real world. I am doing just that and life is coming together very well. We are able to transform in every moment. Currently I am both a rebel and trying to become more zen. We are always both and that balance is difficult to find but find it we must for peace of mind.

Please read my next book **Chilled Demons – Cheeky Heroes** to follow my progress.

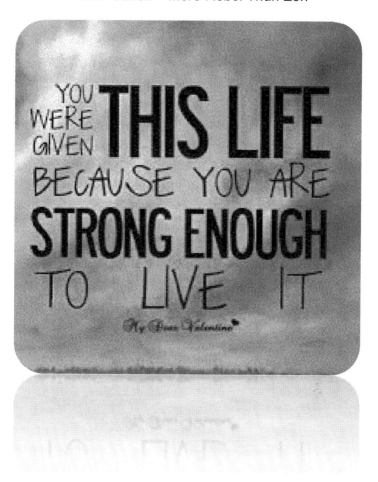

YOU WERE GIVEN **THIS LIFE** BECAUSE YOU ARE **STRONG ENOUGH** TO LIVE IT

Peace & Love – Adam x

Getting Better

Top Personal Development Books @
www.AdamSenex.com

Top Personal Development Blog @
www.MoreRebelThanZen.com

Life Coaching @ **www.Soul2Whole.com**

Physique Fitness & Nutrition @
www.TheGreatBodyBible.com

Getting Better Books @
www.GettingBetterBooks.com

Adam Senex – Getting Better Series

Book 1 – Dazed & Confused

Book 2 – More Rebel Than Zen

Book 3 – Chilled Demons Cheeky Heroes

Book 4 – Sometimes I Pretend To Be Normal

Book 5 – Coming Soon……..

also

The Great Body Bible - The Fitness Wizards
available from www.authorhouse.co.uk

Feeding The Active Body - Gary Walsh

Made in the USA
Charleston, SC
01 August 2016